Geoff Hamilton's

RadioTimes

GARDENING YEAR

Geoff Hamilton's
Radio Times
GARDENING YEAR

Geoff Hamilton and Sue Fisher

BCA

LONDON   NEW YORK   SYDNEY   TORONTO

This edition published 1994
by BCA
by arrangement with Network Books
Network Books is an imprint of BBC Books,
a division of BBC Enterprises Limited

CN 8461

DESIGNED AND TYPESET BY
Bob Gordon Design

ILLUSTRATIONS BY
Karen Cochrane

Set in Caslon and Franklin Gothic

PRINTED AND BOUND IN GERMANY BY
MOHNDRUCK GRAPHISCHE BETRIEBE GMBH, GÜTERSLOH

PICTURE CREDITS

Network Books would like to thank the following for providing photographs and for permission to reproduce copyright material. While every effort has been made to trace and acknowledge all copyright holders, we would like to apologise should there have been any errors or omissions.

Liz Eddison pages 39, 115 (Chelsea 1990), 123 (Chelsea 1993), 163; **John Glover** pages 14, 26, 43, 50-51, 55, 66-67, 86, 87, 103, 146, 179; **Melvin Gray/NHPA** page 81; **Jerry Harpur** pages 15, 34, 59, 130, 131, 147, 166-167; **Neil Holmes/The Garden Picture Library** page 154-155; **Andrew Lawson** pages 54, 138-139, 142, 159, 170, 174-175; **Clive Nichols** pages 18-19, 22, 23, 30-31, 38, 46, 63, 74-75, 77, 79, 83, 94-95, 99, 106, 107, 110-111, 114, 119, 126-127, 143, 150, 178; **The Harry Smith Collection** pages 47, 98, 151B, 158.
All other photographs by **Stephen Hamilton**.

CONTENTS

Climate map 8

Introduction 9

CLIMATE MAP

It's quite impossible to forecast the beginning and the end of winter accurately, but these maps will give a good idea of the climate in your area. They show the average dates of the last and first screen (air) frosts. All frost-tender plants should be protected or brought inside a week or so before the date of the first frost of the winter and no plants should be planted outside until a good week after the predicted last one. Plants put out into slightly warmer conditions will always catch up, so it's much better to err on the side of caution. Remember too that seeds sown in cold soil could rot.

AVERAGE DATE OF LAST SCREEN FROST
- before March 1
- during March
- during April
- during May
- after May 30

AVERAGE DATE OF FIRST SCREEN FROST
- after November 30
- during November
- October 16–31
- October 1–15
- before October

INTRODUCTION

GARDENERS ARE FOREVER looking ahead. Well before we've harvested our first runner beans of the summer for example, we have to be thinking about sowing cabbages for winter. Just as we're enjoying the late summer dahlias and chrysanthemums, we must turn our minds to ensuring a fabulous show of daffodils and tulips for the following spring. It's terrific fun, but it takes a bit of planning.

Naturally, with the benefit of nearly forty years of experience, it becomes almost a matter of habit. I could no more forget in June to sow the chicory for forcing in January than you could forget to put your foot on the clutch before you changed gear. It becomes automatic.

Mind you, that's not to say that I don't still make mistakes or that I'm not still learning. Of course I am. And I know that even after all these years I wouldn't be without the security of a dog-eared, worn and very grubby notebook that records past seasons and serves to jog my memory.

So I thought it would be a good idea to share that notebook with you, plus a wealth of extra advice and experience from my friend Sue Fisher. We think we've covered most of the jobs you'll be needing to do through the year to produce a beautiful and productive garden, plus a few ideas and projects you might not have thought of.

But one of the major problems with this type of book is that gardening by the calendar is really not the best way to do it. Naturally, seasons vary. I've known snow in the south of England in the first week in June when even the most cautious gardeners were planting out their tender bedding. And I've seen April rain in Scotland simply wash plants from the soil and float them away!

So treat this book as a guide and memory jogger, but always remain flexible. Vary your timings according to the season and, of course, where you live. The climate map will help there.

And don't be afraid to stick your neck out. Sometimes nature smiles on the adventurous. A non-gardening friend, for example, once asked me if he could shift his roses in August when the weather was dry and they were in full bloom. As you would expect, I laughed scornfully. None the less, he went ahead and blow me if every single one didn't survive. Three weeks later they were blooming again. I couldn't recommend that you go that far unless, as in his case, it's essential.

But above all, never let your garden worry you. Do that, and you defeat the whole object of gardening. It's there to be enjoyed and, if you work along with nature, it's guaranteed to give you the greatest creative fulfilment you could find anywhere. I do hope that this book will help you to achieve just that.

JANUARY

GARDENING is all about optimism. In the cold dark days of January, when icy winds chill you to the marrow, you may think that all outdoor work should be consigned to the back burner until the weather improves. Not a bit of it!

In fact it's one of the most exciting months of the year because there's so much to look forward to. At the end of the month the first spring bulbs will break through and buds on trees and shrubs will start to fatten. Spring really is just around the corner.

Best of all, however, the end of January sees the first of the seeds going in. Sure, it's a nail-biting time and, even after a lifetime of gardening, I still feel that good old tingle of excitement and yes, surprise when the first green shoots push through. And from now on, of course, it just gets better and better all the time.

◀ *The winter garden has a still, ethereal beauty when all the bare twigs are silvered with frost.*

GARDENS TO VISIT

- **Glasgow Botanic Gardens**, Strathclyde. Huge glasshouses with many tropical plants, especially orchids, begonias and tree ferns. Many attractive landscaped areas outside.
- **Royal Botanic Gardens, Kew**, Surrey. Huge range of features including Palm House and Princess of Wales conservatory for winter interest. Many other plantings for year-round colour. Shop, café and restaurant.
- **Tatton Park**, Cheshire. Formal gardens surround the nineteenth-century house (open), including Japanese garden. Woodland gardens look best in spring/early summer.
- **Trebah**, Cornwall. Superb ravine garden on Helford river, originally planted 1850s. Water garden with huge *Gunnera*. Many rare and exotic trees and shrubs including tree ferns.

Looking good

The month of January can often seem interminable, but there's a surprising number of attractive plants that give the winter garden and your spirits a real lift. For maximum enjoyment plant them so that they can easily be seen from indoors, or near the main pathways and entrance to your house. With a bit of colour in the garden it seems as though spring really isn't too far away at all.

Winter-flowering shrubs make a wonderful show. Most are deciduous and produce flowers along their naked stems – most flowers are also sweetly scented, and a few sprigs cut for a vase will perfume a whole room.

Wintersweet (*Chimonanthus praecox*) bears deliciously scented, pale yellow flowers. Witch hazels (*Hamamelis* varieties) are magnificent large shrubs that bear spidery tassels of yellow or reddish flowers which are often scented, and the hazel-like leaves also colour well in autumn. Bear in mind, though, that they do best on neutral to acid soils.

Shrubby honeysuckles (*Lonicera fragrantissima*, *L.* x *purpusii* and *L. standishii*) also produce delectably fragrant creamy yellow or white flowers. *Viburnum* x *bodnantense* and *V. farreri* varieties bear clusters of pink or white scented flowers.

V. tinus varieties produce flat heads of white or pink-tinged flowers. This species is evergreen, so it is particularly useful for giving structure to a border, and even makes a good informal hedge. Christmas box varieties (*Sarcococca*) bear creamy-white tassels of flowers which give off a strong vanilla-like scent.

Flowering trees are unfortunately a rare sight at this time of year, in fact the best winter-flowering tree is the autumn cherry (*Prunus subhirtella* 'Autumnalis'), which bears many clusters of flowers from early winter right through to spring. There is also a pink-flowered form, *P. s.* 'Autumnalis Rosea'.

Shrubs and trees with coloured stems make an invaluable contribution to the winter garden. Snakebark maples (*Acer davidii*, *A. grosseri* var. *hersii* and *A. pensylvanicum*) have bark that is prettily patterned in green and white. Some birches (*Betula* varieties) have gleaming white bark, especially *B. jacquemontii*. Dogwoods such as *Cornus alba* varieties and *C. sanguinea* 'Winter Flame' have bright red or orange stems – to encourage plenty of coloured stems, hard prune in early spring (see page 42). Tibetan cherry (*Prunus serrula*) has glossy mahogany-red bark: plant this tree where the winter sun will shine on the bark for the best effect.

THE GARDEN INDOORS

INDOOR COLOUR FROM THE GARDEN

Winter temperatures don't encourage sitting outside and admiring the garden for long, so enjoy your plants to the full by bringing some of the garden into the house. A vase of winter flowers from the garden has more charm and appeal than expensive florists' flowers, and often has the added bonus of scent too. All the winter-flowering shrubs and trees mentioned on this page can be used – simply cut a few stems well-furnished with flowers, crush the cut ends to help water uptake and put them in a vase of water.

Hellebore flowers are beautiful but need a little more preparation to last well in water. Use a pin to prick through the length of the stem at 1 cm (½ in) intervals, or slit the stem completely up one side. This helps the flowers take up sufficient water to last for a week or so. Stems of early spring-flowering shrubs such as flowering quince, forsythia, flowering currant and cherries can be coaxed prematurely into flower indoors. Again, cut a few well-budded stems and crush the ends, then put them in a deep vase or jug full of very hot (but not boiling) water in a reasonably warm room. Within a short time you'll have a blaze of spring colour indoors while winter still holds sway outside.

General tasks

Shrubs and herbaceous plants that have been recently planted should be checked and firmed in if necessary. Frost can lift the ground around the roots, and wind can rock the stems, allowing water to lie on the crown of the roots and so causing rotting. Stake plants that are moving about too much.

Check staked trees to ensure that their ties are not over-tight or are rubbing the plant. In extreme cases a plant can be permanently maimed or even killed by incorrectly fixed ties.

Clean pots and seedtrays with hot water and household bleach ready for use in spring. This is a fairly tedious job but a very useful one – dirty seedtrays can harbour pests and diseases, and in spring you'll want to get on with sowing your seeds without having to clean all your containers first.

Dig heavy ground so long as the soil isn't too wet, and leave it rough in large clods. Frost will break them down and make the soil more workable in the spring. Annual weeds can be buried in the ground during digging, but the roots and leaves of perennial weeds should be removed and destroyed.

Moss can make paths and patios dangerously slippery. Clean paving and concrete using a stiff brush and a paving cleaner. On compacted gravel paths, moss and algae can be dispersed by raking and loosening the gravel.

Mowers and tools should all be checked and sent for servicing if necessary. Don't leave it until spring when the repair shops will be overwhelmed and you may have to wait some time.

Order seeds and summer-flowering bulbs from mail-order suppliers before they begin to sell out.

PLANTING A TREE

1 *Put the stake in before putting the tree in the hole. Use the shaft of your spade to check the tree is planted at the same level as it was previously.*

2 *Backfill the soil around the tree, treading down firmly to make sure there are no air pockets left around the roots.*

3 *Secure the tree to the stake using a wide plastic tree tie. Check the tie occasionally to make sure it isn't cutting into the trunk.*

Plant deciduous trees, shrubs, fruit and roses if the ground is not over-wet and there are no severe frosts (see pages 144 and 160). If you must plant in frozen soil, dig off the frozen layer and put it to one side to replace later.

Snow can cause damage to shrubs and conifers by weighting down, distorting and even breaking branches, particularly upward-pointing ones. Garden structures can also be at risk. Knock snow off gently using a broom, but leave it undisturbed if there is no danger of damage – it makes a very good natural insulator.

Weeding and maintaining borders is ideally done now when there's a bit of room to move between plants, but only if the soil is dry enough not to turn to mud when you tread on it. Dig out both annual and perennial weeds – compost annual weeds, but burn or dispose of the roots of perennial weeds.

Once the ground is clean, very lightly fork the bare soil between the plants and spread a layer of well-rotted manure or compost. Alternatively, cut down on weeding in the future by spreading a 5-cm (2-in) thick mulch of chipped bark on the soil.

Tibetan cherry (Prunus serrula) *has beautiful mahogany-coloured bark that gleams in the winter sunlight. Plant this tree near a pathway because its bark is irresistible to touch.*

Ornamental garden

CLIMBERS

Prune young wisteria shoots (with the exception of the main leader shoots) back to within 7.5 cm (3 in) of the previous year's growth.

HERBACEOUS PERENNIALS

Winter-flowering perennials such as Christmas rose (*Helleborus niger*) and *Iris unguicularis* should be starting to produce clusters of buds, and putting cloches over them will protect their flowers from the ravages of winter weather. Both plants produce exquisite blooms that can be cut for indoor decoration.

LAWNS

Aerate a lawn suffering from poor drainage, which becomes apparent if water lies for any length of time after rain. Push in a garden fork about 15 cm (6 in) deep and rock it backwards and forwards to enlarge the holes. Repeat at 15-cm (6-in) intervals. Immediately afterwards, brush in sharp sand. If the drainage problem is severe, use a hollow-tine fork which can be bought or hired. This removes plugs of soil, and the resulting holes should then be filled with sharp sand as above.

Lay turf for a new lawn if the ground is not frozen or too wet to be workable. See page 149.

SHRUBS

Pot-grown shrubs benefit enormously from protection during winter. Because the entire plant is above ground, the roots are very vulnerable to frost damage, especially if there is no snow around to provide natural insulation. To protect the plants put the containers close together, ideally against a wall. Then wrap protective material such as bubble polythene or hessian sacking around the pots. Alternatively wrap them with ordinary polythene and stuff a layer of straw between it and the pot sides.

WATER GARDEN

Ice forming a solid layer for more than a couple of days causes toxic gases to build up underneath. Either melt a hole gradually by standing a pan of boiling water on the pond, or in the autumn put a ball in the water to keep a small area ice-free. Never break ice with a sharp blow.

PLANT OF THE MONTH

Winter jasmine *(Jasminum nudiflorum)*
HEIGHT: 1.8 m (6 ft)
SPREAD: Up to 1.8 m (6 ft)
FLOWERING TIME: November – March
POSITION: Sun or shade
SOIL: Any except very poor soils. **HARDY?**: yes

Winter jasmine brightens up the dullest winter days with golden-yellow stars of flowers strung along its naked branches. This is a wonderfully accommodating plant that is happy in a wide range of aspects, soils and uses. Train it on wires against a wall or up a post, pillar or pergola. Immediately after flowering prune all long straggly growths to around 5 cm (2 in) to maintain a bushy shape and encourage plenty of flowers next winter.

Kitchen garden

FRUIT

Fruit trees and bushes, especially black currants, should be covered with netting where practicable, to protect the buds from hungry birds. Put out a selection of seeds, nuts and scraps for the birds instead. Don't forget that birds are our allies, eating large quantities of greenfly, caterpillars and many other pests, so you want to keep on the right side of them!

Stored fruit should be checked regularly. Throw out any with signs of rot, or it will spread rapidly to the others.

VEGETABLES

Brassicas, like broccoli, Brussels sprouts, cabbage, cauliflowers and kale, are a feast for hungry birds in midwinter, so protect crops with netting. Lift stumps after harvesting and add them to the compost heap, shredding them first if possible or bashing them with a hammer to speed rotting.

Broad beans and peas can be sown outside if you live in a mild area or have a light soil. Alternatively put out cloches now to warm the soil and sow in a couple of weeks. Sow broad beans in double rows 10 cm (4 in) apart, with 1 m (3 feet) between double rows. Sow peas in double rows 15 cm (6 in) apart with 7.5 cm (3 in) between plants.

Prepare ground for spring sowing by covering it with clear polythene or setting out cloches four to six weeks before sowing. This warms the soil, gets seeds off to a flying start and helps prevent them rotting in cold, wet ground. Soil protected like this is also more workable, so the seedbed can be easily and thoroughly prepared. In addition the first flush of annual weeds germinates and can be hoed off before crops are sown, so there's less competition and fiddly weeding later. This is called the 'stale seedbed' technique and is widely used by commercial growers.

▲ *Check stored apples every couple of weeks. Take out any showing signs of rot or it could spread through the whole bag.*

▶ *Cover the ground with clear polythene a few weeks before sowing to get seeds off to a flying start. Weigh the edges down well with timber or bricks.*

Greenhouse and windowsill

Bulbs stored in the dark for forcing (see page 181) should be regularly inspected.

Potted bulbs that have finished flowering, except specially prepared hyacinths, can be planted outside. First move them to a cool but light situation, remove their dead flowerheads and allow the leaves to die back naturally. Feed with a high-potash fertilizer and water regularly but sparingly until the leaves have yellowed and died back. In spring the bulbs, complete with compost, can be taken from their pots and planted out in the garden.

Sow lettuce in the unheated greenhouse or coldframe. Choose a variety that has been bred especially for this purpose, such as 'Fivia' or 'Kelly's'.

Fungal diseases are more likely to appear during the winter months when ventilation has to be restricted. Good greenhouse hygiene greatly helps, but remember that you can't cure fungus diseases; you can only avoid them. So pick off and remove dead or faded leaves, and space established plants to allow air movement around the foliage. Botrytis or grey mould is a very common fungal disease that appears as a fluffy grey mould on any part of the plant above soil level. Remove all affected parts and spray with copper fungicide.

Stored tubers and corms of begonias, dahlias, gladioli and other plants should be checked regularly for disease. Remove any showing signs of rot, which would otherwise quickly spread through the entire batch.

Ventilate the greenhouse on mild or sunny days, but do remember to close up again in mid-afternoon when the temperature starts to fall sharply. If you're heating the greenhouse with gas or paraffin, there should be a small amount of ventilation all the time.

Wash the outside of the greenhouse and frame to admit as much light as possible during these short days – you'll be surprised how much grime has accumulated on apparently clean glass!

Water plants sparingly: water requirements are much reduced in winter, and over-watering can lead to disease or even death of plants. Feed only plants that are in flower using a liquid fertilizer once a week.

EARLY VEGETABLES

Push a table up to the window in the spare room, or anywhere where there's a little warmth, and, towards the end of the month, start off some vegetables.

Fill four 7.5-cm (3-in) pots with coir compost and sow an early lettuce variety, spinach, summer cauliflower and summer cabbage. When they're big enough, they can be transferred to seedtrays and grown on.

In modules (seedtrays divided into a number of cells) sow radishes, onions, salad onions and round carrots, putting six to eight seeds per cell. Do the same with turnips and beetroot, but sow only two seeds per cell. These will be planted out under cloches just as they are, without thinning out (see page 46).

At the same time sow a 7.5-cm (3-in) pot with radishes and grow them on the windowsill for the earliest fresh veg. of the year in about six weeks.

CHECKLIST

- Continue planting trees and shrubs if weather permits.
- Clean out the bottoms of hedges.
- Keep on top of weeds like groundsel and chickweed which continue seeding even in winter.
- Mulch rhododendrons to protect the roots from frost.
- Sow seeds of alpines and trees which need a cold spell before germinating.
- Continue pruning apple and pear trees (see page 180).
- Bring potted strawberries inside for forcing.
- Pot up a few lily-of-the-valley for flowering indoors.
- If you heat the greenhouse, start off geraniums from seed.
- Test your soil for acidity and correct with lime if necessary.

FEBRUARY

FEBRUARY can be a difficult month for working outside but it's certainly the most optimistic of the whole year. Wind, rain, snow and ice can keep even the hardiest gardener indoors. It really does more harm than good to work on soaking-wet soil, which soon becomes muddy. That drives out air, destroys its structure and makes it quite difficult to bring back into 'working order' when it does dry out. It's best to keep off it and, if there are things you must do, work off boards.

However, there's plenty to keep you occupied in the greenhouse with last month's sowings needing transplanting and plenty more sowing to do this month too.

The garden also really starts to come alive with spring bulbs pushing through and the occasional flash of colour to get you excited.

*◀ The scarcity of flowers in late winter makes these snowdrops and Lenten roses (*Helleborus orientalis*) even more precious. They can be used to brighten up any shady spot, especially under large shrubs.*

GARDENS TO VISIT

- **Aberdeen Duthie Park and Winter Gardens**. Conservatories filled with exotic plants, collection of cactus, birds and fish. Spectacular summer floral displays, Japanese garden, alpines and water features.
- **Benington Lordship**, Hertfordshire. Magnificent carpets of snowdrops and winter-flowering shrubs. Terraced garden, lakes, rose garden, herbaceous borders.
- **Ness gardens**, Cheshire. Botanic gardens of University of Liverpool. Winter garden and heathers, superb collections of lime-hating shrubs. Many other plants for year-round interest.
- **Rosemoor Garden**, Devon. RHS garden. Variety of plants and themed gardens including alpines, herbs, potager, bog garden and roses. Shop, restaurant and plant centre.

Looking good

Winter-flowering plants are still at their peak this month, and though they might have been battered by severe winter weather, they'll come smiling through. February can be blessed with mild sunny days that give the flowers a new lease of life. The first blossoms of spring are starting to appear now, along with a few sleepy bees and other insects on warmer days.

Shrubs testing the water with a few tentative blooms include camellias, with their beautiful waxy flowers. These garden aristocrats have an undeserved reputation for tenderness – although their glossy, dark green leaves can be scorched by hard frosts, they're hardy plants and do well both in tubs and borders. There are many different-coloured hybrids of *Camellia japonica* and *C.* x *williamsii*, so it's best to choose a plant in flower to be certain of buying exactly the right colour. Then again, they're all good. *Rhododendron* 'Praecox' is one of the earliest rhododendrons to flower, producing masses of bright rosy-purple blooms. Though camellias and rhododendrons do need an acid soil, the more compact varieties can be grown in containers of lime-free compost.

There are no such problems with mahonias. They're excellent plants for year-round impact with large, handsome, evergreen leaves, and spikes of fragrant yellow flowers from now until well into spring. For a contrasting bright splash of colour, mezereon (*Daphne mezereum*) produces purple-red fragrant flowers all along its naked stems, followed in autumn by bright red, poisonous berries. It'll fill the garden with exotic perfume.

There's a surprising number of shrubs that are looking really good at this time of year. Winter jasmine (*Jasminum nudiflorum*) is still covered in golden starry flowers, and other winter-flowerers like the deliciously-scented wintersweet (*Chimonanthus praecox*) and Cornelian cherry (*Cornus mas*) are still going strong. *Garrya elliptica* makes a wonderful show right through winter with tassels of huge catkins – male varieties, such as 'James Roof', give the best display.

Herbaceous perennials in flower are rare in February, but those few are worthy of a place in any garden. Christmas rose (*Helleborus niger*) produces glistening white blooms as early as December until late winter, when it's joined by the Lenten rose (*Helleborus orientalis*) with beautiful nodding flowers in many shades from white to reddish-purple. The Lenten rose flowers until April, and its evergreen foliage provides good winter interest too, but cut off the old leaves now to show the flowers at their best. Hellebores prefer a shady site, unlike *Iris unguicularis*, which needs a sun-baked position in order to produce its stunning blue flowers. Lungworts (*Pulmonaria*) are happy in sun or shade, and their flowers are just starting to open now. Clumps of blue- and white-flowering pulmonarias planted together make a wonderful colour contrast. The first sweet violets (*Viola odorata*) begin to open their sweetly-scented flowers in sheltered corners.

Bulbs are the real forerunners of spring and will lift your spirits sky-high. By now the green shoots of many varieties promise a glorious show once spring gets into its stride, and some of the smaller bulbs are already providing drifts of colour. These include the earliest crocuses like *Crocus ancyrensis*, *C. chrysanthus* and *C. tomasinianus*, with yellow, white, blue and purple flowers; *Iris danfordiae* and *I. reticulata*, with delightful yellow and blue flowers; *Anemone blanda*, which bears beautiful sky-blue flowers and looks wonderful planted in masses, as does winter aconite (*Eranthis hyemalis*), with bright golden flowers; and of course snowdrops (*Galanthus*) with their pearly-white nodding flowerheads. All these small bulbs are ideal for planting in groups or drifts under trees and shrubs, or they can be naturalized in grass. Make a note to plant some later this spring or next autumn.

Winter-flowering pansies are perfect partners for bulbs, though they make a lovely show just by themselves. Plant them in autumn in tubs or borders where they can be seen from indoors, and they'll flower in all but the hardest weather right through until spring.

THE GARDEN INDOORS

Grow your own Pot Plants

If you have a heated greenhouse or a sunny windowsill, you can grow your own flowering pot plants to fill the house with colour most of the year – and at a fraction of the cost of ready-grown plants. Make a succession of sowings so they don't all mature at once.

Begonias and gloxinias can be bought now as tubers and half-buried in trays or small pots of compost at a temperature of around 13°C (55°F) – don't plant them any deeper or the tubers could rot. Plant begonia tubers hollow side uppermost. When the shoots are around 2.5 cm (1 in) high, transfer them into 13-cm (5-in) pots and grow them on in plenty of light. Water as needed by putting the pot into a saucer of water for an hour or so, as surface water can lie on and rot the tuber. Feed weekly with a liquid fertilizer.

Browallia, Coleus, Exacum, Gerbera, winter cherry (*Solanum capsicastrum*), Cape primrose (*Streptocarpus*) and black-eyed Susie (*Thunbergia alata*) can be grown from seed. Gloxinias can also be grown from seed as well as from tubers. Sow at 18°C (65°F) and, when they're big enough to handle, pot the seedlings into small pots. Once they're well rooted, pot them on into their final 13-cm (5-in) pots.

Some annuals, like *Clarkia, Salpiglossis* and butterfly flower or poor man's orchid (*Schizanthus*), can also be grown as pot plants. Sow seed at a temperature of 16°C (61°F), prick out the seedlings into small pots and finally pot three plants into a 13-cm (5-in) pot. For really cheap and cheerful houseplants, do the same thing with annual bedding like petunias, busy Lizzies and antirrhinums.

Begonia tubers can be started into growth in a warm room or greenhouse. Plant them with the hollow side up.

General tasks

Crocuses and dwarf daffodils like Narcissus cyclamineus *are ideal for naturalizing in grass, where they can be planted to make glorious drifts of colour.*

Prune overgrown deciduous hedges as early in the month as possible, before birds begin to nest. Prune the hedge 30–60 cm (1–2 ft) lower than the height you actually want, as young shoots will quickly grow from the top. When trimming the sides, it is best to shape the hedge so that it is narrower at the top and wider at the base.

Prepare trenches for runner beans and sweet peas, which need a good moisture-retentive soil to crop well: your efforts now will pay dividends later. Choose a sunny site and dig out a trench two spades deep. Half-fill it with material that holds moisture well, like screwed-up newspaper and kitchen waste, then refill with soil. Don't forget to mark its position for when you come to plant in spring.

Weeding and maintaining borders should be completed this month before easily damaged new shoots develop on shrubs and perennials (see page 169).

Ornamental garden

ANNUALS

Sweet peas can be sown outside 1 cm (½ in) deep. To speed germination and protect emerging seedlings, cover the seed with a 'cloche' made from the top half of a large plastic bottle with the cap removed.

BULBS

Lilies will be coming into the garden centres now. Avoid bulbs that have been shrivelled in the sun and stick with fat juicy ones. They prefer moisture-retentive, well-drained soil that's rich in organic matter, so dig in plenty of compost or manure. Improve the drainage of heavy soils by adding coarse grit, and put each individual bulb on a small mound of grit in the planting hole. Plant so that the bulbs are covered with about 10–20 cm (4–8 in) of soil, preferably in groups of three or five. The one exception is the madonna lily (*Lilium candidum*) which is planted with its top just below the surface. If the soil's not in good condition, pot the bulbs to plant out later.

Snowdrops and winter aconites establish best if bought and planted immediately after flowering (or 'in the green', as it is known). Planting dry bulbs in the autumn is rarely successful. Specialist nurseries supply bulbs in the green by mail order, and garden centres sell pot grown plants.

Overcrowded clumps of bulbs should be dug up carefully with a fork, separated into smaller clumps and replanted immediately at the same depth at which they were growing previously.

CLIMBERS

Small-flowered clematis that flower in late summer – *Clematis orientalis, C. texensis* and *C. viticella* varieties – should be hard pruned towards the end of the month. Prune each stem back to 23–45 cm (9–18 in), cutting to a pair of strong healthy buds. These clematis are ideal to

PLANT OF THE MONTH

Christmas box (*Sarcococca hookeriana* var. *digyna*)
HEIGHT: 60 cm (2 ft)
SPREAD: 45–60 cm (18 in–2 ft)
FLOWERING TIME: December/January – March
POSITION: Sun or shade
SOIL: Any except chalky soils **HARDY?**: Yes

This compact evergreen is one of the very best shrubs for winter interest. It has a neat strong shape that attracts the eye, forming an upright clump of stems clothed in pointed, dark green leaves. The small creamy-white tassels of flowers aren't very showy, but they have a delightful and penetrating scent. Make the most of the fragrance by planting it near the back door, next to a pathway, or in a border or tub. Alternatively you could grow it in a pot and, when it flowers, bring it into the porch or an unheated greenhouse to flood it with fragrance.

23

TAKING ROOT CUTTINGS

1 *Dig up a plant like this oriental poppy (*Papaver orientale*) and shake or wash the soil from the roots. Cut off an entire root near the crown of the plant.*

2 *Cut the root into sections 5 cm (2 in) long, making a slanting cut at the lower end so you know which way up to put them.*

3 *Dust the pieces with fungicide powder and push them, sloping-end down, into pots of coir compost.*

grow through climbing roses, as both plants can be pruned at the same time.

Large-flowered clematis that flower in mid to late summer, such as 'Elsa Späth', 'Henryi', 'Marie Boisselot' and 'William Kennett', should be pruned at the same time. Remove all thin weak stems, and prune the remaining ones back by around a third to a strong pair of buds. It's a good idea to prune some stems more and others less, so that the plant will produce flowers from top to bottom.

Summer and winter jasmines (*Jasminum officinale* and *J. nudiflorum*) should now be pruned. Weak, dead and damaged shoots should be removed from both varieties. Thin overgrown plants of summer jasmine by removing some of the older branches completely, either at ground level or where they join the main stems. Don't just shorten the stems or you'll encourage masses of weak bushy shoots.

Winter jasmine should be pruned immediately after flowering. Shorten all side shoots and long straggly growths to within 5 cm (2 in) of the main stems to encourage a bushy habit and plenty of flowering shoots next winter.

HERBACEOUS PERENNIALS

Root cuttings can be taken of selected perennials, including bear's breeches (*Acanthus*), *Anchusa*, perennial forget-me-not (*Brunnera macrophylla*), Cupid's dart (*Catananche*), bleeding heart (*Dicentra*), sea lavender (*Limonium*), oriental poppy (*Papaver orientale*) and tree poppy (*Romneya*).

Take cuttings as described (left) and then put the pots in a coldframe, or stand them in a sheltered place outside and cover them with cloches. When growth starts, pot up the cuttings individually and grow them on to get them well established before planting out, usually the following year.

LAWN

Aerate a lawn suffering from poor drainage (see page 15).

Cut an established lawn for the first time during mild weather if growth has started, and provided, of course, that it's dry. Do remember to set the mower blades higher than usual for the first two or three cuts of the season. Before mowing, brush the grass with a stiff broom to scatter worm casts, or you'll end up with lots of little flattened patches of soil which are ideal seedbeds for weeds.

Rake out the 'thatch' (or layer of dead grass) in the lawn in spring to allow light, air and water through to the roots. Use a springtine rake for small areas, or hire a powered raking machine for larger lawns.

Remove lawn weeds by digging them out with a narrow trowel or an old knife, or by using a special tool which twists the whole weed out of the ground. Alternatively use a chemical weedkiller – provided the weather is mild and dry; if it isn't, wait until next month.

Prepare ground for a new lawn to be sown or turfed in spring. This advance groundwork is all-important to allow the soil to settle. The groundwork should be just as thorough for turfed lawns as for those grown from seed.

Start by digging a hole two spades deep, just to check whether there's a hard layer underneath. If there is, you will need to break up the whole area by double digging, to make sure that the lawn won't be forever wet. Otherwise, single digging or rotavating is enough. On heavy clay soils, add some coarse grit to improve the drainage. While digging, mix in about a barrowload of grit to 3 sq. m (3 sq. yds). Leave the ground rough to settle for several weeks. See page 38 for the final preparation.

Instead of a traditional grass lawn, you might want to consider a few alternatives. For an informal area a wild-flower lawn of grass and native flowers is gloriously colourful, attracts lots of useful insects and needs little maintenance. It should be cut only once in late spring and again in mid-summer, so that the flowers can set seed. A mown grass path through

it gives easy access, and also shows that the long grass is part of a definite design rather than neglect! A small area that's little used could be planted with thyme or chamomile to make a delightfully fragrant, low-maintenance lawn, though both plants need a well-drained soil. Choose the varieties *Chamaemelum nobile* 'Treneague' (chamomile) and *Thymus serpyllum* (creeping thyme).

All shrubs benefit from a spring application of slow-release fertilizer like pelleted chicken manure.

CREATE AN EXOTIC BORDER

Never waste the storage-heater effect of a south-facing wall. If you improve the drainage, you'll be able to grow exotic tender plants you never thought would survive.

Improve the soil at the base of the wall by digging in quantities of coarse grit. Don't be tempted to use sharp sand, which could actually make drainage worse: use pea shingle about 2 mm in diameter.

If the border's wide, you may like to set a few stepping stones in the soil to make a path. You can grow spreading plants alongside and between the slabs to make an attractive feature.

You'll want to experiment with all kinds of tender plants, but don't start until all danger of frost has passed in June. That gives them a chance to acclimatize before next winter. After planting, mulch round the plants with coarser gravel which will store even more heat during the day and release it at night. It also shows off the plants to perfection.

Finally, insure against winter losses by taking cuttings in August and over-wintering them in the cold greenhouse or on the windowsill. Most plants can be propagated in this way.

SHRUBS

Pot-grown shrubs benefit from top dressing with fresh potting compost. Remove the top few centimetres of old soil, taking care not to damage the roots, and replace it with compost to which you have added a slow-release fertilizer.

Protect containers during severely cold spells of weather (see page 15).

Thin out overgrown evergreens by removing entire branches either where they join the main stem, or at ground level. Only hardier evergreens like Laurel (*Prunus laurocerasus*) should be pruned now. Those varieties that are susceptible to frost damage such as Mexican orange blossom (*Choisya ternata*) are best pruned in summer (see page 64).

Camellia japonica *'Lady Clare'* is just one of the many camellia varieties that makes a glorious spring splash of colour. If you notice that the leaves of your camellia start to turn yellow between the veins, give the plant a feed of sequestered iron or an acid fertilizer.

Kitchen garden

FRUIT

Autumn-fruiting raspberries should be pruned now: cut the canes right down to ground level.

Feed established fruit trees, bushes and soft fruit with pelleted chicken manure or blood, fish and bone meal. If you're a non-organic gardener, use rose fertilizer because it has a high potash content that'll give fruiting a boost. All fruit trees and bushes will really benefit from a good mulch of compost or well-rotted manure too. Make sure that the ground is free from weeds first.

Protect peaches, nectarines and almonds against peach leaf curl. This fungal disease appears during summer as reddish puckered patches that distort whole leaves, and it often devastates the entire tree. Rain spreads the disease spores, so protecting small trees with a physical barrier of polythene or other material from now until late spring should stop infection. Chemical control is not so effective. Spray with copper fungicide and apply a second spray two weeks later. If you regularly have bad attacks, grow a dwarf tree in a pot and keep it under cover until June.

Rhubarb can be forced for an early crop. A terracotta forcer looks very attractive, though a large bucket or small dustbin does the same job. Put some loose straw in the container for added warmth and place it over a clump of rhubarb in the garden. The first sticks should be ready for harvest in around six to eight weeks. You'll be surprised at the milder, more delicate flavour. Rhubarb plants should be at least two years old before forcing, and should not be forced again for several years to let them recover.

Strawberries can be forced for an early crop: cover them with cloches towards the end of the month. Ideally plants should be only a year or so old, as older plants tend to produce too much foliage. Make sure that the cloches are ventilated at each end, and when the plants are in flower, take a few cloches away during the day to let the pollinating insects in.

VEGETABLES

Early potatoes are best sprouted (or 'chitted') in advance of planting next month. They'll grow away quickly and give a bigger yield. Buy seed potatoes and set them out in boxes, trays or old egg boxes, with the end containing the most 'eyes' uppermost. Stand them in a light, airy, frost-free place.

Feed overwintered vegetables, including asparagus beds, applying a balanced general fertilizer.

Plant out Jerusalem artichokes and shallots. Plant artichoke tubers in single rows 15 cm (6 in) deep and 30 cm (1 ft) apart. Plant shallots 15 cm (6 in) apart in shallow drills 30 cm (1 ft) apart, pushing them into prepared ground so that the nose of each bulb is just visible.

Prepare seedbeds by covering the ground with clear polythene (see page 16). Apply a general fertilizer two weeks before sowing.

Sow vegetables under cloches or outdoors in milder areas, including beetroot, carrots, lettuce, spinach, turnips, cauliflowers, radish and salad onions. Sow broad beans and peas outside. See page 27 for spacings.

Deep beds are ideal for growing vegetables on heavy soils. The drainage and fertility are improved and there is no problem with soil compaction. Deep beds are also easy to cover with clear polythene or cloches for a very early start. They should not be dug when the ground is wet (see page 130).

Greenhouse and windowsill

Hardy annuals can be grown quickly and easily from seed to make a stunning border for next summer, for no more than a few pounds. The easiest way is to wait until next month and sow direct outside (see page 36) – but you can get a head start by sowing in seedtrays now in an unheated greenhouse or coldframe. The best way to grow them is to sow a tiny pinch of seeds in each cell of a modular tray . They'll make really bushy plants which can be planted out without thinning. You can also grow cheap and cheerful hardy annuals as cut flowers (see The Garden Indoors page 53).

Dahlias and chrysanthemums stored over winter should now be brought into growth so that cuttings can be taken from the new shoots. Put the potted tubers in full light, water well and spray with water regularly. Newly bought dahlia tubers can be treated in the same way.

Dahlias provide spectacular colour from mid-summer until the first frost, and they're also good for cut flowers. There are many different forms to suit all

Dahlia tubers can be bought now, potted up and brought into a warm place. Cuttings can be taken from the new shoots.

tastes – vivid and tall cactus varieties, pompons and decoratives for borders and cutting, dwarf anemone-flowered forms with unusual double centres, and simple, single-flowered mignon dahlias. The dwarf forms are particularly good for tubs.

Take cuttings by removing shoots when they're 7.5–10 cm (3–4 in) long. Use a sharp knife to cut just below a leaf joint and then cut off the lower leaves. Dip the entire cutting into liquid fungicide (wear gloves for this or have a good scrub afterwards), dip the base into hormone rooting powder, and put it into a pot of compost made with equal parts of coir compost and horticultural vermiculite. Place the pots in a propagator or in a polythene bag, ideally with a little bottom heat to maintain a temperature of 10–13°C (50–55°F).

Busy Lizzie (*Impatiens*) can be tricky to grow. The seed can't be covered as it needs light to germinate, though it also needs a constantly humid atmosphere. The answer is to draw very shallow drills in the compost, sow the seed in these drills and cover them with a thin layer of fine vermiculite, which holds lots of moisture and still lets light through. Put the pots or trays in a propagator or cover them with glass or polythene to keep the moisture in, at a temperature of 21°C (70°F).

Lilies can be potted and grown in an unheated greenhouse or a coldframe to get an early start before you plant them out into tubs or borders, or they can be planted directly into tubs Use long pots and plant the bulbs 10 cm (4 in) deep.

Strawberries that were potted the previous summer for forcing (see page 135) should be brought into the greenhouse if they weren't moved in last month. Feed them with a high potash fertilizer and water regularly.

Sweet peas should be sown by the end of the month for best results. To speed germination, soak the seeds in tepid water overnight to soften their hard coats. Sow them 1 cm (½in) deep in special sweet pea tubes or deep pots, sowing one seed per tube or several per pot. Keep at 15°C (60°F) until the seedlings appear, then grow them on in a cold-frame, an unheated greenhouse, or on a cool light windowsill.

Tender perennials that have been over-wintered, including fuchsias and marguerites (*Argyranthemum*), can now be brought into growth. Repot the plants into fresh compost, prune them back, water well and spray with water frequently to encourage growth.

Cuttings that were rooted last summer/autumn into small pots should be potted on into 13-cm (5-in) pots, using coir compost with a little slow-release fertilizer added. Tap the young plants out of their original pots very gently to avoid damaging the roots.

Tomato plants can be sown either in a heated greenhouse or on a warm windowsill with a temperature of around 18°C (65°F) from the middle of the

month onwards. Sow the seed thinly in trays and cover it lightly with sieved compost or vermiculite.

Ventilate the greenhouse as often as possible and for increasingly longer periods during mild or sunny days to help prevent fungal diseases. If signs of disease do appear, treat as described on page 17.

Sweet peas provide a beautiful long-lasting display of scented flowers and are easy to grow from seed.

CHECKLIST

- Continue planting trees and shrubs if weather permits.
- Prick out vegetables sown last month (not module-sown ones).
- Bring in any remaining bulbs being forced in pots.
- Complete the pruning of apple and pear trees this month (see page 180).
- Cut back dead stems of herbaceous perennials to ground level.
- Take basal cuttings of *Anthemis tinctoria*.
- Start sowing half-hardy annuals (see page 47).
- Check that all tools and machinery are in good working order.
- Finish cleaning pots and seedtrays ready for sowing.

- Divide and pot up single pieces of Michaelmas daises (*Aster novi-belgii*). Grow them on and plant out in April.
- Firm in recently planted shrubs and trees if loosened by weather.
- Put out regular supplies of food and water for birds.
- Stock up on pots, compost, labels, twine and other sundries.
- Water tubs and wall-trained plants if necessary.
- Cut back woody stems of mahonias to encourage new growth.
- Test your soil for lime and dress if necessary.

MARCH

THIS IS IT. The gardener's spring arrives in March and it heralds the beginning of the best few months of concentrated enjoyment you could possibly imagine. Make sure that you get started in the vegetable plot with a few onions and shallots, and ideally put out some cloches to grow the earliest salads too. Even a few large cut-off plastic bottles will do to get them going.

By the end of the month all kinds of vegetable can go in and it's time for sowing seeds of hardy annual flowers. The latter are about the best value for a gardener – they're easy to grow and guaranteed in just a few months.

The clocks go forwards too, so we have some extra daylight. You're going to need it and I'll bet that, once you get started, you won't want to come in until you can't see what you're doing.

◄ *Bulbs fill the spring garden with drifts of colour. Plant them amongst shrubs and other plants in borders so the dying foliage will be concealed.*

GARDENS TO VISIT

- **Durham Botanic Garden,** County Durham. Lots of winter colour including heather beds and tropical glasshouses. Many attractive plantings for all-year interest.
- **Exbury Gardens,** Hampshire. Famous ericaceous plants including the Rothschild collection of azaleas, plus magnolias, camellias and rhododendrons. A pageant of colour from early spring to summer. Plant centre, shop and café.
- **Trewithen Gardens,** Cornwall. Much of the garden is superb woodland plantings with shrubs like magnolias and camellias which have reached tree-like proportions. Especially good from early spring to early summer.
- **Younger Botanic Garden,** Strathclyde. Part of the Royal Botanic Garden, Edinburgh. Magnificent woodland garden with conifers and other trees. Over 250 species of rhododendron. Many flowering shrubs in spring/summer.

Looking good

This month sees the winter-flowering shrubs go out in a blaze of glory, but the first spring flowers are even more determined to show their class. The natural world wakes up and stretches itself to the welcome of masses of bright and cheerful blossoms from bulbs, perennials, shrubs and trees.

Trees are just starting to open their blossoms. The first ornamental flowering cherry trees herald the real blaze of colour that comes next month. These earlier varieties include *Prunus* 'Pandora', a small tree covered in masses of shell-pink flowers, the Yoshino cherry (*P. x yedoensis*) with white, pink-flushed flowers, and *P. sargentii* which has bright pink flowers and excellent autumn leaf colour too. *P. triloba* 'Multiplex' forms a large shrub and bears masses of double pink flowers; this variety does especially well when grown against a wall.

Shrubs that flower in spring include many with vibrant colours. *Forsythia* varieties are easy to grow and are immensely popular – and no one should regard 'popular' as bad. They're much-loved because they're excellent reliable plants, which always produce masses of bright yellow flowers before their leaves appear. *F.* 'Lynwood' forms a large bush, though 'Gold Tide', 'Weekend' and 'Arnold Dwarf' are much more compact. For a more subtle shade try *F. suspensa*, which has paler yellow flowers and can be trained to grow against a wall.

Flowering quinces (*Chaenomeles*) perform best when they're trained against a wall or fence, though they can also be grown free-standing. These tolerant plants are happy in sun or shade and produce many flowers along their naked stems, followed by edible fruits in autumn. Choose from many varieties in shades of red, pink or white, like 'Nivalis' (white), 'Moerloosei' (pink and white), 'Umbilicata' (salmon-pink), or 'Crimson and Gold' (deep crimson with gold anthers in the centre). A new variety, 'Lemon and Lime', is white in bud before opening its unusual pale yellow and green flowers. If you want the best edible variety, choose 'Vranja', though you may have to go to a fruit specialist to get it.

Mahonias are now well into their stride. There are lots of varieties to choose from, all of which produce fragrant yellow flowers. *Mahonia aquifolium* 'Smaragd' and 'Apollo' are compact and they're good for small spaces. 'Buckland', 'Winter Sun' and 'Lionel Fortescue' are taller and more imposing. They're ideal structure plants for the back of the border. *M. lomariifolia* has very attractive, divided leaves, but it's not as hardy as other varieties and needs a sheltered spot.

Herbaceous perennials like leopard's bane (*Doronicum*) with its bright yellow daisy flowers, the primula 'Wanda' which bears deep claret-purple ones, and the spotted leaves and pink, red or white flowers of the lungworts (*Pulmonaria*) are ideal for planting under summer-flowering shrubs like hardy fuchsias and tree mallow (*Lavatera olbia*). These shrubs are virtually non-existent now after they have been pruned, but they grow into large bushes later in summer. Perennials with year-round, bold, handsome foliage deserve a more prominent position, such as elephant's ears (*Bergenia*) with its rounded evergreen leaves and clusters of white, pink or red flowers. *Hellebore* species with their beautiful unusual flowers also are attractive even when they're not in bloom. All these perennials are tolerant of partial or even total shade, and one of the best for such conditions is barrenwort (*Epimedium*). Its delicate heart-shaped leaves form a carpet of different shades of green and red, and they're complimented by small spikes of red, yellow or white flowers. Our native primrose, *P. vulgaris*, with its delicate creamy-yellow flowers, tends to look rather shy against all the brighter colours in the spring garden, though there are few plants that look lovelier and more appealing during this season. Primroses are most at home in a woodland setting, so plant them under trees along with other native wild flowers like the sweet violet (*Viola odorata*), bugle (*Ajuga reptans*), cowslip (*P. veris*) and drifts of snowdrops to create a beautiful spring scene.

Bulbs are now starting to make a tremendous show. It's hard to have too many bulbs – they can be tucked into so many different places in the garden: tubs, hanging baskets, under deciduous shrubs and hedges, or just in clumps or colourful drifts.

The earliest daffodils and narcissi are starting to make an appearance – tall varieties include 'Fortune', 'Brunswick', 'St Keverne' and 'Dutch Master'. Dwarf cyclamineus narcissi have delicate flowers with swept-back petals: look for 'February Gold', 'Jenny', 'Peeping Tom', 'Jack Snipe' and 'Tête-à-Tête'. Plant these little beauties in tubs, raised beds or on rockeries to appreciate them fully (see page 132).

The first dwarf tulip species are also starting to flower. They lack the rigid formality of the taller varieties and blend well with informal border plantings or in tubs. Make a note for next autumn to plant some *Tulipa kauffmaniana* hybrids like the salmon-orange 'Shakespeare', and 'Stresa' with its unusual bi-coloured red and yellow flowers.

The smallest bulbs are best planted in massed groups to provide drifts of colour. If your borders look a little bare at the moment, remind yourself to plant some in September or October. As well as crocus and snowdrops, there are Grecian windflower (*Anemone blanda*) with dainty blue or pink flowers, pale blue glory of the snow (*Chionodoxa*) and, of course, the deep blue bluebells (*Scilla sibirica*). Dwarf iris like the yellow-flowered *Iris danfordiae* and blue *I. reticulata* need a well-drained soil and are ideal for rockeries, as are the tiniest narcissi like *N. minimus*.

THE GARDEN INDOORS

WINDOWSILL SALADS

A warm windowsill is all you need to produce a selection of deliciously crisp and fresh salad vegetables right through the year.

Sprouting seeds are the easiest and quickest of all salad veg. — they're ready in under a week and they taste wonderful. Simply put a handful of seed in a large glass jar, cover it with water and fix a piece of muslin over the top of the jar. All you need to do is rinse the seed twice daily with fresh cold water, and within a few days you'll have a good helping of crunchy sprouts that are delicious in salads and stir-fries. They'll also keep for up to four days in the refrigerator, stored in a polythene bag. Varieties of seed for sprouting include aduki beans, salad alfalfa, mung beans (Chinese bean sprouts) and fenugreek.

Mustard and cress is also simple to grow on the windowsill. Just spread the seed evenly on several layers of moist kitchen paper in the bottom of a plastic sandwich box and watch it grow.

In 7.5-cm (3-in) pots, sow a few seeds of lettuce, salad rocket and radish to add the final touch to your salads. A cut-and-come-again variety of lettuce like 'Salad Bowl' is best, so you can harvest a few leaves at a time.

Catkin-bearing trees and shrubs are amongst the loveliest of spring flowers. Willows (*Salix*) produce many different and very beautiful catkins, like the delicate, soft grey 'pussy willows' of the Kilmarnock willow (*Salix caprea* 'Pendula') which forms a compact weeping tree. *S. hastata* 'Wehrhahnii' and *S. lanata* make small bushes which are ideal for restricted spaces. Look out for less usual varieties like *S. aegyptiaca*, a large shrub bearing bright yellow catkins, and *S. gracilistyla* with probably the best catkins of the lot (they're grey at first, later turning yellow).

The hazels (*Corylus*) also bear attractive catkins. The unusually-shaped corkscrew hazel or Harry Lauder's walking stick, (*C. avellana* 'Contorta') makes a large shrub with curiously twisted branches and it's festooned with long catkins in early spring. Bees enjoy feeding on the dusty yellow pollen that catkins produce.

After the long winter, the first spring flowers, like these clumps of Narcissus *'February Gold', the starry, purple* Anemone blanda *and the pinky-mauve lungworts (*Pulmonaria*), bring the garden to life.*

General tasks

Sow green manure crops on areas of soil that will be left bare through the summer. They keep down weeds, stop valuable nutrients being washed out of light soils, their roots help break up heavy soils, and later the whole crop is dug in to add nutrients and improve the soil structure.

Varieties to sow include alfalfa, buckwheat, crimson clover, fenugreek, mustard, phacelia and trefoil. They can be sown from now until August, and there are several other varieties to sow during autumn (see page 144).

Mulch the bare soil in borders and around trees with a 5-cm (2-in) thick layer of organic matter like well-rotted manure, garden compost, spent mushroom compost, chipped bark, cocoa-shells, or garden shreddings that have been stacked for six months. A mulch helps to suppress weeds and improves the soil, and it looks good too.

Don't use mushroom compost around acid-loving (lime-hating) plants as it contains some lime.

Plant evergreens that are susceptible to frost damage to give them plenty of time to establish before next winter. In the coldest areas delay planting until next month. Varieties that prefer spring planting include Californian lilac (*Ceanothus*), Mexican orange blossom (*Choisya*), sun rose (*Cistus*), hebe, daisy bush (*Olearia*), New Zealand flax (*Phormium*) and wall germander (*Teucrium*). Such plants prefer a sunny sheltered site and good drainage as they hate having wet roots in winter.

A mulch of well-rotted garden compost really benefits all plants. Fork it lightly into the bare soil taking care not to damage newly emerged shoots.

Ornamental garden

ANNUALS

Hardy annuals can be sown in rows or irregularly shaped patches outside. There are many varieties that can provide a wealth of cheap and cheerful colour throughout the summer, including Californian poppy (*Eschscholzia*), *Godetia*, night-scented stock (*Matthiola bicornis*), love-in-a-mist (*Nigella*), Iceland poppy (*Papaver nudicaule*) and snapdragon (*Antirrhinum*). For further information on sowing and varieties see The Garden Indoors, page 53.

Annual wild flowers make a glorious show of colour, and unlike most garden plants, many varieties love a poor gravelly soil in a sunny site. Try centaury, corn marigold, corncockle, field poppy, larkspur, pheasant's-eye and wild pansy. Sow the seed thinly in patches and rake

Primulas and polyanthus are best divided after they've flowered, once they've formed fairly large clumps. Either replant the divisions directly into the border or, if you want them for next year's spring bedding schemes, line them out in a nursery bed until the autumn.

it into the soil lightly. These plants will do better without fertilizer.

Vegetables are often relegated to the furthest corners of the garden, but they are just as ornamental as flowers – and you can eat them too. Seed producers are introducing a whole new generation of ornamental vegetables. Try the looseleaf lettuce with red leaves 'Lollo Rosso', Swiss chard 'Ruby' with glowing red stems and green leaves, yellow-podded French beans like 'Neckargold' and 'Goldperle', yellow-fruited courgettes like 'Gold Rush', and sprouting broccoli with yellow or purple heads. See pages 70 and 72 for details of how to grow them.

Where space is limited, try some of the new 'mini-vegetables'. They've been specially selected because of their suitability for being grown closely together and for eating when they're young. Varieties include cauliflower 'Idol', courgette 'Supremo', squash 'Sunburst', beetroot 'Monaco' and leek 'King Richard.

Sweet peas sown last autumn in pots can be planted out. Plant them in prepared trenches full of water-retentive organic material (see page 22), or dig plenty of compost into the soil. Sweet peas can also be sown outside now.

Before sowing or planting, set out their supports. Bamboo canes and netting are ideal, or use twiggy branches ('pea sticks'), or cylinders of stiff plastic netting if you're growing them informally in mixed borders. If you want them for cutting, set them 15 cm (6 in) apart in double rows 30 cm (1 ft) apart. Slugs love newly planted seedlings, so protect them with collars cut from clear plastic bottles.

CLIMBERS

Clematis that flower in late summer should be pruned at the start of the month if they were not done earlier (see page 23).

Overgrown ivies should be trimmed as required. Stems in the wrong place that are clinging tightly to wood or brickwork should be cut and left for several weeks. This lets the aerial roots shrivel a bit so that they cause less damage when removed.

HERBACEOUS PERENNIALS AND ALPINES

Rockeries and alpine beds should be thoroughly weeded, and any new planting should be done now too. Afterwards, spread a fresh layer of coarse grit around the plants. Most alpines dislike excess moisture and this keeps the foliage off the soil, sets the plants off well and helps prevent more weed growth.

Herbaceous perennials will benefit from division and replanting every three or four years, especially where they've formed large clumps, or when the centre of the plant is becoming bare. Division can be done at any time during the winter, though autumn and early spring are best. In most areas of the country this month is the time to start.

First dig up the entire clump using a spade or fork, then split it in one of two ways, depending on the type of roots. Those with woody roots are best divided by pushing two garden forks back to back into the clump, then levering them apart to break it up. Fleshy-rooted plants are best cut into pieces with a large knife, and each piece should consist of several shoots with plenty of root. In both cases get rid of the old woody centre of the clump. A few plants, like hostas, can be sawn into pieces with an old tenon saw or a bread knife; the pieces with a visible bud can then be replanted.

Replant the divisions in groups to give a natural appearance, into soil which you have revitalized by digging in compost or manure and some general fertilizer. Firm the plants well and water them in.

Tall-growing perennials benefit greatly from early support – don't leave it until summer when the stems are actually collapsing. Support clump-formers like

phlox with a tailor-made wire frame or grid put over the plant so that the stems grow through it. A circle of canes and twine, or pea sticks, also make good supports, while taller plants like delphiniums can be supported individually with bamboo canes. Tie in as they grow.

Slugs attack new shoots and are especially partial to delphiniums, hostas and ligularias. Surround the crown of each plant with a good layer of sharp grit, and scatter a little slug bait if absolutely necessary. As temporary protection for small, new plants, cut collars from clear plastic bottles to put round them until they've grown large enough to withstand a little slug damage.

A biological slug control has recently become available. It's a nematode (a microscopic worm) which can be bought in little sachets from garden centres or by mail order. To apply it, mix the contents of the sachet with water, and simply water it onto a given area using a watering can. The nematode only attacks and kills slugs and it's effective for around six

Early support for tall-growing perennials pays dividends later in the year because it helps the plant to retain its shape and form.

37

***Daphne odora* 'Aureomarginata'**
HEIGHT: 1-1.2 m (3-4 ft)
SPREAD: 1 m (3 ft)
FLOWERING TIME: February–April/May
POSITION: Sunny and sheltered
SOIL: Moisture-retentive and well-drained.
HARDY?: In all but the coldest areas.

Noted for its exquisitely perfumed flowers, this variety is also an excellent plant for year-round interest. It forms a loose dome of glossy evergreen leaves narrowly edged with white, and produces many small clusters of reddish-purple flowers that begin to open in late winter and often last through most of spring. Their intense fragrance is not unlike a strong lily-of-the-valley scent. Little pruning is needed: just cut out any dead or overcrowded shoots after flowering. Propagate by half-ripe cuttings in late summer.

weeks. However, it isn't cheap, so make sure you use it where your plants need the most protection.

LAWN

Mow an established lawn during mild weather. Set the mower blades higher than usual for the first cut, gradually lowering them over the next two or three. Before the first cut of the year, use a stiff broom to scatter worm casts, and repeat whenever necessary before mowing.

Rake out the 'thatch' (layer of dead grass) if you didn't do it earlier (see page 25).

Tackle lawn weeds if you're a gardener who worries about them. Either dig them out by hand or, as a very last resort, use a selective lawn weedkiller. Take great care to follow the manufacturer's instructions and be absolutely sure that none of it gets on your borders or you'll kill your plants.

Feed the lawn with a granular or a liquid fertilizer. The best way to put on a granular fertilizer is with a special distributor to be sure of the correct coverage. It *must* be watered in, so if it hasn't rained within two days following application, it's essential to water the lawn thoroughly.

Ground preparation for a new lawn should be finished after the initial digging (see page 25). When the soil's reasonably dry, roughly level the ground with the back of a fork, filling in and firming any large hollows. Then tread over the whole area to ensure that every centimetre is evenly firmed. This is the most important part of the whole job. If it sinks later, you'll end up with an uneven lawn that's scalped by the mower on the bumps and full of coarse grass in the hollows.

Clear any perennial weeds while levelling. If lots of annual weeds have grown

▶ *Containers planted with spring bulbs and flowers in the autumn give a magnificent display without needing much maintenance.*

Pruning bush roses

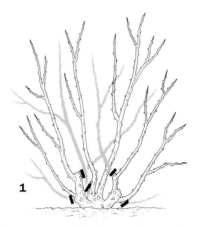

1

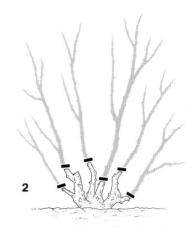

2

up between cultivating and levelling, hoe them off on a dry day.

Apply a general fertilizer at the rate of around one handful per sq. m (sq. yd). Then rake the soil level, removing large stones and filling in any little hollows as you go. Take your time over this. Step back every so often, crouch down and squint across the surface. From that angle you'll be able to see where the unevenness lies.

Many different seed mixes are available. A mix containing rye grass is much the best for most purposes. It makes a good general-purpose lawn that'll stand a fair amount of wear and tear. Bear in mind that a 'bowling green' sown with fine seed needs lots of maintenance (like mowing *every* day!) and cannot be used very much.

Sow seed at around 50 g per sq. m (1½ oz per sq. yd), which is about two handfuls. To be a little more accurate you could weigh this amount first and mark out a square metre to see what the correct amount of seed looks like on the ground – though really, there's no need to worry too much about exact rates; pinpoint accuracy isn't vital. When in doubt, err on the generous side.

Scatter the seed evenly by hand, then rake the ground lightly using a springtine rake so that about half the seed is covered with soil. Birds love a ready-prepared meal of lawn seed, so try to keep them off using home-made bird-scarers – strips of foil or cut-up plastic compost

bags strung on lines of string between low posts to shake and rattle in the wind. Unless the weather is unseasonally hot and dry, it's best not to water until after germination, or the seed will be washed into uneven groups.

Turfing can actually be done at any time of year, weather and soil conditions permitting (see page 149).

SHRUBS
Roses can now be pruned, including rambler roses that were not pruned after flowering last summer (see page 133).

Rose pruning is necessary to develop a vigorous, healthy, well-balanced plant with plenty of flowers. Removing excessive growth lets plenty of light and air around the plant, which helps prevent disease and encourages healthy growth.

When starting to prune, first remove completely dead, diseased and damaged wood. Then do the formative pruning.

Always use sharp secateurs that cut cleanly, and a small pruning saw for thicker branches. Buds will grow in the direction they're facing, so cut back to just above an outward-facing bud so that the shoot it produces grows out and up rather than into the centre of the plant.

Hard pruning helps increase vigour: weak shoots should therefore be cut back hard and strong ones not so hard. Anything really weak and spindly should be removed completely. Put on an organic or a rose fertilizer after pruning.

Pruning shrub roses

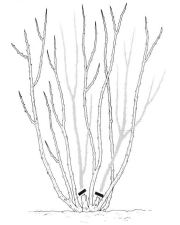

Pruning climbing roses

Bush roses – large-flowered (hybrid tea) and cluster-flowered (floribunda) roses. First remove all the weak shoots and those growing towards the centre of the plant (**1**). Then cut strong shoots back to within 5–7.5 cm (2–3 in) of last year's growth, and weaker shoots to within 2.5 cm (1 in) (**2**).

Shrub roses. Remove about a third of the oldest and thickest branches right near ground level to encourage the plant to produce new growth from its base.

Climbing roses. The main stems form a permanent framework of branches and flowers are borne on the side shoots, which should be cut back to two or three buds. Prune out a proportion of the main branches if the plant is outgrowing its site. After pruning, tie in branches, pulling them down towards the horizontal to restrict the flow of sap and encourage flowering.

Standard roses. These are just large-flowered and cluster-flowered roses on a taller stem, so they should be treated in the same way.

Eucalyptus gunnii should be pruned towards the end of the month. Cut the whole plant hard back to within 15 cm (6 in) of the ground, which encourages fresh shoots with attractive, rounded, young foliage. Unpruned eucalyptus that have developed into straggly trees can still be cut back to the same height – it looks drastic but most plants recover.

Late summer-flowering shrubs should also be pruned towards the end of the month, including butterfly bush (*Buddleia davidii*), blue spiraea (*Caryopteris*), *Ceratostigma* and flowering nutmeg (*Leycesteria*). Cut plants back hard, leaving around 5 cm (2 in) of last year's growth.

Lavatera olbia and hardy *Fuchsia* varieties should be cut back totally to within 7.5–15 cm (3–6 in) of the ground, to where new growth is beginning to show. In colder areas delay pruning until you can see that new growth, which may be next month.

Pruning late summer-flowering shrubs

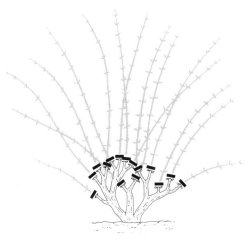

LAYERING SHRUBS

Layering is a reliable way of propagating many shrubs, and it can be done from spring to late summer. The shrub in the pictures is *Aucuba japonica* 'Speckles'.

1 *Choose a branch which is reasonably young, supple and near the ground. With a sharp knife, wound the stem by taking a small sliver of bark from the underside.*

2 *Wounding the stem helps stimulate root formation, which is further encouraged by putting a little hormone rooting powder into the cut.*

3 *Mix a little potting compost into the soil underneath, and securely peg down the stem with wire.*

Shrubs with coloured stems like dogwood (*Cornus*), *Rubus* and shrubby varieties of willow (*Salix*) should be hard pruned towards the end of the month. Do this by cutting all the shoots back to within 15–30 cm (6–12 in) of the ground, or to the trunk if there is one. On heavy or poor soils where the plant is growing less strongly, prune only every other year to avoid weakening the plant. This hard pruning encourages plenty of new, straight, brightly coloured stems.

Winter-flowering heathers should be lightly trimmed with shears once flowering has finished to encourage neat and bushy growth.

WATER GARDEN

Start to feed fish as the weather begins to warm up. At this time of year their appetites can vary depending on the temperature, so take care not to over-feed. Just give enough food to be eaten in a couple of minutes, otherwise it'll pollute the pond. Over-feeding is a major cause of green water, because microscopic green algae feed on the surplus nutrients. Alternatively supply a live food like *Daphnia* (water fleas), which simply live in the pond until they're eaten.

Feed pond plants that aren't growing well using tablets of slow-release aquatic plant fertilizer. Simply push a tablet into the soil around each plant's roots to feed it for the whole season. There's no need to feed floating or oxygenating plants as they'll take sufficient nutrients from the water.

Submersible pumps stored over winter can now be reconnected and put in the pond, and pool heaters can be removed.

▶ *The earliest water-garden plants to flower are kingcup (*Caltha palustris*) which has bright gold flowers, and* Lysichitum americanum *with its unusual yellow spathes. Both plants grow happily in shallow water or very boggy soil.*

Kitchen garden

FRUIT

Apricots, cherries and peaches flower early and their buds are susceptible to frost damage, so protect wall- or fence-trained trees with fleece or polythene. Fix a sheet to a couple of long poles which can then be leaned against the wall or fence. In the day time, roll it up.

There are few insects around to pollinate the flowers this early in the year, so it's worth hand-pollinating them using a small soft paintbrush to transfer pollen by just touching it on the open blossoms.

Continue to protect peaches, nectarines and almonds against peach leaf curl (see page 27).

Briar fruits such as blackberries, loganberries and tayberries should be trained and tied in regularly to their supporting wires as they grow. Briar fruits crop on last year's growth, and they're best trained by separating last year's canes to the left and the new growth to the right. This makes pruning in summer much more straightforward and less painful. Above all, keep on top of the job or the fast-growing shoots will get away.

Pests and diseases should be treated with preventative sprays this month, if you use chemical controls. Spray apples and pears against scab when the flower buds are still closed, and again when the buds begin to burst and show colour. Pear trees that have suffered from regular attacks of pear midge should be sprayed with permethrin when the buds are white but still closed. Apple and pear suckers that feed on the flower buds can be destroyed with systemic insecticide.

Do not spray insecticides once the trees are in flower or you'll kill the insects that are essential to pollinate the flowers. However, in my entirely organic garden I *never* spray and have few problems.

Weed all fruit crops, as weeds compete for valuable nutrients. They're much more easily removed at this time of year, especially from among strawberries, cane fruits and prickly gooseberries.

HERBS

Buy and plant pot-grown perennial herbs, including curry plant, mint, rosemary and tarragon. Mint can be very invasive and rapidly spreads by shoots that are just below the surface of the soil, so restrict growth by planting it in a large bucket with the base removed: it can be sunk into the ground out of sight.

Sow hardy varieties of herbs outside, in rows or patches, including chervil, chives, dill, fennel, marjoram and parsley. In colder areas or to get plants off to a flying start, sow under cover.

Fan-trained fruit trees like this pear are easy to grow and can be protected conveniently from frost.

VEGETABLES

Lime vegetable soil if necessary. The correct level of lime lets plants take up the maximum amounts of nutrients from the soil. First test the soil using a cheap and simple kit available from garden centres. The amount of lime present is measured in pH levels. The optimum level for most crops is pH 6.5, so add lime if it's too acid (pH 6.0 or less). The exceptions are for potatoes, which dislike excessive lime, and all members of the cabbage family, which like a very limy soil with a pH of around 7.2 (that'll also help prevent clubroot).

Sets (tiny onions) can be planted now for summer harvest, and seed can be sown for a late summer/ autumn harvest. Sets are more expensive, but they're a reliable way of growing a good crop in a shorter time, and are particularly useful on heavy soil and in colder parts of the country where the growing season is short.

Plant sets in rows 30 cm (1 ft) apart with 7.5 cm (3 in) between individual onions, in drills deep enough so that only the tips can be seen after refilling. After planting check the sets regularly and refirm if required, as they can often be lifted by frost or pulled out entirely by foraging birds. Sow seed in shallow drills 30 cm (1 ft) apart. Onions can also be sown under cover (see page 49).

Thin autumn-sown onions (see page 136) to 5 cm (2 in) apart, and feed with a balanced general fertilizer if you didn't do so last month.

If space is limited, grow a quick-maturing crop like lettuce or radish between rows of onions.

Potatoes set out to sprout last month can be planted at the end of the month. Plant early varieties with the sprouts facing upwards, 15 cm (6 in) deep and 30 cm (1 ft) apart in rows 60 cm (2 ft) apart. Maincrop varieties go in 38 cm (15 in) apart in rows 75 cm (2½ ft) apart.

Potatoes can also be grown under black polythene. Lay polythene on the cultivated and fertilized soil, burying the edges. Cut slits at the recommended intervals and plant through them with a trowel as deeply as you can reach. This method has the bonus of suppressing weed growth, though slugs can be a problem, so scatter slug bait before laying the polythene.

'Earthing up' is the traditional way of protecting potatoes from frost. When the shoots are around 23 cm (9 in) high, use a draw hoe to pull the soil up to their tips. Cover the crop temporarily with fleece if a severe frost is forecast.

Seeds of many vegetables can be sown now in milder areas. In colder areas or on heavy wet soils, delay sowing until next month, or sow vegetables under cover (see page 17). In these cases cover and prepare seedbeds in advance (see page 16).

FRUITS FOR SMALL PLACES

If you have only a tiny garden, you can still grow your own orchard by taking advantage of the walls or fences. Fan-trained apples and pears look really attractive, are easy to prune and will produce quite large crops. You can now buy trees already fan-trained and with a built-in pollinating variety as well.

All apples and pears need another variety to pollinate them so that they produce a full crop of fruit. You therefore have to buy either two trees or one of these fan-trained specials. Known as 'family-fans', they have two or sometimes three different varieties grafted on one plant.

As you would expect, the varieties have been chosen to ensure good pollination and to give a succession of picking. The difficulty is making sure that one variety is not so strong that it takes over from the others.

To guard against this, the growers have taken advantage of the fact that the more vertically a branch grows, the more vigorous it becomes. So the strongest varieties are put at the bottom of the fan, where they'll be trained out horizontally, with the weakest in the middle where they'll grow vertically. The result is a perfectly balanced tree.

Start by fixing horizontal wires to the wall or fence at about 45 cm (18 in) apart. Plant the tree against the wall or fence and then wire bamboo canes on to the wires in a fan arrangement. Fix the branches to the canes with soft string and the job's done. For pruning see page 135.

Vegetables to sow now include broad beans, carrots, leeks, lettuce, parsnips, peas, radish, salad onions, salad rocket, spinach, Swiss chard and spinach beet. Make regular sowings every two to three weeks to ensure a steady supply.

Towards the end of the month, Brussels sprouts, kale, red cabbage, summer cabbage and summer cauliflower should be sown in a prepared seedbed, which ideally should have a pH of around 7.2 – add lime if necessary.

Vegetables sown in January in modules should be planted out under cloches. Plant the cells complete – no thinning is required. Space carrots 15 cm (6 in) apart; beetroot, onions and turnips 30 cm (1 ft) apart, salad onions and radish 7.5 cm (3 in) apart.

At the same time, sow under cloches: beetroot, kohl rabi, summer cabbage and cauliflower, carrots, radish, spinach, turnips and, at the end of the month, French beans.

Greenhouse and windowsill

Amaryllis (*Hippeastrum*) bulbs should be watered regularly as required and fed weekly with a liquid feed. Continue watering and feeding after flowering has finished so that the bulb builds up its reserves for next year.

Begonia and gloxinia tubers can still be planted (see page 21). Tubers planted last month should be potted on into 13-cm (5-in) pots when they have produced shoots 2.5 cm (1 in) high.

Damping-off disease often attacks young seedlings. This fungal disease becomes apparent when clusters or entire trayfuls of seedlings collapse, as a result of the stems shrivelling and turning brown at soil level. Good air movement helps prevent it, so ventilate the greenhouse whenever possible and sow seeds thinly. Water early in the day so that the seedlings don't stay wet, and for the same reason water them from below by placing trays and pots in water rather than watering from above.

If damping-off disease does appear, remove affected seedlings and water the remaining ones with copper fungicide. If necessary, throw out the entire trayful.

Pests often start appearing this month, so monitor plants and their environment carefully. Yellow 'sticky traps' can be hung near plants – insects are attracted to the bright colour and become trapped. They're particularly effective against whitefly.

Whitefly are tenacious greenhouse pests that can begin to appear now. They may also be controlled organically with a predatory wasp, *Encarsia formosa*, which you should be able to buy through the garden centre or by mail order.

An unconventional but effective method of control is to use a domestic vacuum cleaner and simply suck up whitefly using the pipe attachment – it sounds crazy but it works!

Biological pest control by introducing the natural enemies of pests is safe and organic, and much better than using strong persistent chemicals, especially as some pests have now become resistant to certain chemicals. Whitefly, red spider mite, vine weevil, and scale insect can all be tackled this way.

For biological control to be successful there does need to be a reasonable number of pests already there, and the predators mostly need a high minimum

Amaryllis (Hippeastrum) bulbs can be kept from year to year, although they do benefit from regular feeding with a high-potash fertilizer.

temperature in order to function, so you can't start too early in the season. Do remember, though, that you probably won't be able to use chemical insecticides simultaneously or you'll kill the useful predators.

Half-hardy annuals can be sown, provided a minimum temperature of 10–13°C (50–55°F) can be maintained.

Ageratum, *Alyssum*, ten-week stock (*Matthiola incana*), tobacco plant (*Nicotiana*) and marigolds (*Tagetes*) need gentle heat of around 15°C (60°F) to germinate.

Lobelia erinus, *Nemesia*, *Phlox drummondii* and *Zinnia* need higher temperatures of around 18°C (65°F).

Varieties that need a long growing season are best sown as soon as possible, such as *Begonia semperflorens*, busy Lizzy (*Impatiens*), *Lobelia* and *Petunia*. If you want only a few plants of a particular variety that needs heat, or one that is hard to germinate, it's often well worth buying ready-germinated seedlings. Many garden centres now sell potfuls of seedlings ready for pricking out, and these often cost little more than a packet of seed.

Tender perennials started into growth last month should have produced new shoots suitable for cuttings. Take cuttings about 7.5 cm (3 in) long, making a clean cut just below a leaf joint. Remove most of the lower leaves, dip the base in hormone rooting powder and push the cuttings into pots of compost. Cover with a propagator lid or polythene bag and keep in a warm shaded place until rooted.

Geraniums that have been over-wintered can now be brought into growth, and cuttings can be taken from the new shoots. Pot them up into fresh compost and water them well. As growth increases, water regularly and feed every ten days with a liquid feed. Take cuttings as described above, and put them into pots of moist coconut-fibre compost mixed with equal parts of sharp sand. Stand the pots in a warm place out of direct sunlight, but don't cover with polythene as the cuttings are very prone to fungal diseases. Water sparingly as growth begins.

Sow seeds of tender perennials like the cup-and-saucer plant (*Cobaea scandens*) and salvias like the beautiful blue *Salvia patens*. Chilean glory vine (*Eccremocarpus scaber*) is a scrambling perennial climber that comes easily from seed and flowers in its first year. Sow the seed thinly and cover with vermiculite, as they need light to germinate.

Many tender plants like marguerites (*Argyranthemum*), fuchsia, geranium, bidens and lantana can be bought as mini-plants (or 'plugs', as they are often termed) ready for potting on, and this is a much cheaper way of increasing stocks than buying larger plants in late spring. However, they must, of course, go into a warm greenhouse.

THE GARDEN INDOORS

SEED-SOWING AND GROWING TIPS

- Use modular trays for sowing root crops and deep rooted vegetables to reduce root disturbance.
- Always use clean trays and pots to avoid spreading pests and disease.
- Firm the compost well, especially into the corners of trays, but take care not to over-firm soilless composts.
- Water the filled trays and pots before sowing, as seeds can easily be washed deep into the compost if watered afterwards.
- Cover trays with glass or polythene to retain moisture, but remember to check them daily and remove the cover as soon as the seeds begin to germinate.
- Some seeds germinate better in light, so instead of covering them with compost use horticultural vermiculite.
- Give seedlings maximum light to avoid their becoming drawn and leggy.
- Handle seedlings carefully when pricking out and planting. The stem is very vulnerable to bruising, so always handle them by the leaves and use a dibber or pencil to loosen the roots.
- Don't water seedlings with cold water straight from the tap, but fill watering cans and leave them in a warm place for several hours. Get in to the habit of doing this immediately after watering, ready for the next day.

Greenhouse vegetables can be sown, provided the temperature can be maintained at around 18–21°C (65–70°F). A heated propagator would be useful and could save you heating the entire greenhouse. Alternatively, should you want to grow only a few plants, it may well work out cheaper to buy ready-grown ones from a nursery later in spring.

Aubergine seed can be sown thinly in trays at a temperature of 21°C (70°F). The seed can be slow to germinate, so don't worry if it takes some time. Prick out seedlings individually into 7.5-cm (3-in) pots as soon as the seed leaves have unfurled fully. Okra and sweet peppers can be grown in the same way.

Cucumbers can be sown two seeds per 7.5-cm (3-in) pot. Push in these large flat seeds 1 cm (½ in) deep and on edge, to avoid water lying on the seeds and rotting them. Remove one of the seedlings if both seeds germinate.

Continue to sow tomatoes thinly in trays, covering the seed lightly with sieved compost or vermiculite. Tomatoes sown last month can be pricked out individually into 7.5-cm (3-in) pots as soon as the seed leaves are fully formed.

Many other vegetables don't need such high temperatures. Even an unheated greenhouse or coldframe gets vegetables like radish, salad onions, lettuce and carrots off to a flying start, though a little heat obviously speeds their growth. An early start under glass shortens the total growing time, which is valuable in colder areas.

Globe artichokes and root vegetables including carrots, onions, spinach and turnips can be sown in modular trays. Sow carrots, onions and salad onions at the rate of six seeds per cell, sow spinach and turnips two seeds per cell, and sow artichokes individually. Seeds sown in modular trays won't need thinning.

Lettuce, cabbage and cauliflower can be sown in seed trays. Prick out the seedlings when they're large enough to handle.

Cuttings can be taken from dahlia tubers when the shoots are 10cm (4in) high.

Peas can be sown in lengths of guttering, or in large plastic bottles which have been cut in half lengthways. When the seedlings are well established, they can be planted out with very little root disturbance: simply slide them out into a prepared hollow in the ground.

CHECKLIST

- Clean greenhouse and frame glass so that seedlings get maximum light.
- Plant snowdrops and winter aconites as soon as possible.
- Finish planting bare-rooted plants.
- Plant fruit trees and bushes by the end of the month, weather permitting.
- Lay growing bags out in the greenhouse for a few days before planting so that the compost warms through.
- Pinch out the tops of sweet peas when they're 10 cm (4 in) high.
- Remove weeds before they start growing strongly.
- Seed bare patches in the lawn and cover with clear polythene until germination.
- Water established greenhouse plants regularly and feed weekly with liquid feed.
- Feed and water amaryllis (*Hippeastrum*) regularly.
- Continue taking dahlia cuttings from potted tubers.

APRIL

THIS IS THE MONTH when all your not-so-keen neighbours will discover the great outdoors. The sun's bound to be shining, the birds will be singing and the garden centres will be *packed*.

Even for us 'proper' gardeners the blood begins to run just that bit faster as the excitement mounts. There are lots of seeds to sow, plants to plant and even the odd few vegetables to harvest: bliss!

There's masses to do, so reserve the evenings to read this chapter. You'll need all the daylight hours you can get for gardening!

◀ *From April onwards, the border displays become more dramatic. Here, rhododendrons and daffodils will look stunning all month.*

GARDENS TO VISIT

- **Anglesey Abbey**, Cambridgeshire. Mix of gardens and parkland, with avenues of trees. Magnificent displays of spring bulbs. Traditional herbaceous borders look best from June onwards. Shop and restaurant, plants for sale.
- **Knightshayes Court**, Devon. Formal structure of old yew hedges around the Victorian house (open) contains an abundance of choice plants. Collections of acers, camellias, rhododendrons, azaleas, alpines, roses and herbaceous plants. Woodland garden. Restaurant, shop, plants for sale.
- **Savill Garden**, Surrey (part of Windsor Great Park). A garden of pools and moisture-loving plants. In spring rhododendrons, azaleas, pieris, magnolias and camellias are a blaze of colour. Shade-loving herbaceous plants from early spring to summer. Roses and hydrangeas in flower from early to late summer. Restaurant and plant centre.
- **Threave Garden**, Dumfries and Galloway. Home of the Threave School of Gardening. Ornamental gardens, fruit, vegetables and glasshouses. Full of colour and interest from spring to autumn. The plantings are laid out to be educational so plenty of useful tips can be gleaned. Visitor centre and plants for sale.

Looking good

There are no problems choosing plants for colour this month.

Flowering trees are laden with blossom now and through to May. Crab apples (*Malus*) are among the best for small gardens because they're reasonably compact, and they have two periods of interest. Their white, pink or red flowers are followed in autumn by colourful fruits which often remain on the tree for months. If space is very limited, choose a compact variety like *M*. 'Royal Beauty' which forms a head of weeping branches, or *M*. 'Evereste' which has a neat conical shape.

There are many flowering cherries which look fabulous when they're in flower but some can be pretty dull for the rest of the year. Make sure that you choose varieties with good spring flowers and the bonus of fiery autumn colour too, like 'Okame' which bears bright rose-pink flowers, and 'Shosar' with single pink flowers and a narrow upright habit.

Varieties like 'Kanzan' and 'Tai Haku' are widely planted, though where space is limited it's worth looking for more compact varieties like 'Asano' with deep pink, double flowers and 'Kursar' with masses of small, rich pink flowers. For an informal garden or a wildlife area there are few trees more beautiful than *P. avium* 'Plena' with its masses of double white flowers.

Other trees in flower include the snowy mespilus (*Amelanchier lamarckii*) that bears clusters of white flowers which combine with the coppery young leaves to make a wonderful show. The foliage develops good autumn colour, especially on acid soils. Ornamental pears (*Pyrus*) also produce white flowers, though the fruits aren't edible. The best one for gardens is the willow-leaved pear (*P. salicifolia* 'Pendula'), a weeping tree with attractive, narrow, silvery-grey leaves. It forms a wonderful, tall mound of glaucous foliage.

Shrubs are now flowering thick and fast, and those like *Forsythia* which started last month are still going strong. This popular yellow-flowered shrub is often paired with the vivid red-flowering currant *Ribes sanguineum* 'Pulborough Scarlet' and 'King Edward VII', though this species does give off a pungent 'tomcat' smell. Other currants well worth trying include 'Brocklebankii' with golden leaves and pink flowers, and 'Tydeman's White' which has pure white ones.

The barberries are invaluable garden plants that thrive in tough conditions and almost any reasonable soil. *Berberis darwinii* has glossy, dark green foliage and masses of orange flowers, while *B*. x *stenophylla* bears yellow or cream flowers. *B. linearifolia* 'Orange King' and *B*. x *lologensis* 'Apricot Queen' are also excellent and deserve to be more widely grown. The brooms (*Cytisus* x *praecox*) are sun-loving shrubs that grow well in chalky well-drained soil. They're covered with masses of fragrant flowers. *C.p.* 'Allgold' has deep yellow flowers, those of *C.p.* 'Albus' are white, and those of the species are rich cream. There's little to beat some of the viburnums for fragrance. *V*. x *burkwoodii*, *V. carlesii* and *V*. x *juddii* all bear large white or pink-tinged heads of flowers that are deliciously perfumed. The latter is a good strong grower and more resistant to attack by greenfly.

Lesser periwinkles (*Vinca minor*) produce their bright blue, purple or white flowers now, but they're also invaluable ground-cover plants for year-round interest. Their long prostrate stems root as they spread to form a carpet of green or variegated weed-suppressing foliage, and they can be used on banks, for underplanting shrubs and trees, or just as ground cover by themselves. If they get over-exuberant, they're easy to hack out with a spade. Add more colour by inter-planting with clumps of bulbs. They make a good combination because, after

GROW YOUR OWN FLOWERS FOR CUTTING

Fresh flowers are the perfect finishing touch for any room, but buying flowers every week can add up to quite a bill, and you may prefer to enjoy your garden flowers in the garden rather than cutting them, so grow a few especially for cutting. A row or two in the vegetable plot are all that's needed.

Many hardy annuals can be raised from seed to provide a cheap and cheerful blaze of colour. On light soils sow in autumn, otherwise sow in spring to avoid the seeds rotting over winter. Sow thinly in rows and thin the seedlings to 10–15 cm (4–6 in) apart.

Some of the best hardy annuals for cutting include pot marigold (*Calendula*), sweet sultan (*Centaurea imperialis*), Cosmos, larkspur (*Delphinium ajacis*), baby's breath (*Gypsophila elegans*), sunflower (*Helianthus annuus*), love-in-a-mist (*Nigella*) and black-eyed Susan (*Rudbeckia*).

Sweet peas are excellent for cutting too. They need to be picked regularly, as leaving seed heads on the plant makes it think that it no longer needs to flower and reproduce itself. See pages 29 and 36 for growing details.

Dahlias are also wonderful for cutting and they flower right through summer until the first frosts. Either buy tubers for planting out this month (see page 60, for details) or pot them under cover and take cuttings from the new shoots (see page 53).

---

flowering, the dying bulb foliage is hidden by the periwinkle. Avoid the invasive greater periwinkle (*Vinca major*) unless you want to cover a large area of ground.

Many lime-hating evergreen shrubs such as *Rhododendron* and *Pieris* are starting to look their best. Though the majority of *Rhododendron* varieties flower next month, some dwarf ones bloom now and are perfect for rockeries, tubs and borders. Good varieties include 'Blue Diamond' and 'Blue Tit' with lavender-blue flowers, 'Chink' which has unusual yellow-green flowers, 'Elizabeth' with dark red ones and 'Ginny Gee' which is pale pink. There's a wealth of different varieties however, so it's well worth selecting plants in flower to get exactly the colour you want. *Pieris* are beautiful plants with attractive foliage, and they produce sprays of little urn-shaped flowers, usually white, that smell deliciously of honey and are popular with bees.

Some varieties like 'Forest Flame', 'Bert Chandler' and 'Wakehurst' produce bright red young growths in spring that look superb against the glossy green adult foliage. These new shoots can be damaged by frost, and it's worth protecting them with horticultural fleece on cold nights. For the best year-round interest, choose a variety like 'Flaming Silver' with variegated foliage.

Corylopsis pauciflora also needs an acid soil. This twiggy, deciduous shrub bears many dangling clusters of creamy-yellow flowers, which have a delicious perfume similar to that of cowslips.

Stachyurus praecox is covered with similarly-shaped pale yellow flowers, though it's not fussy about soil. It forms a substantial bush which is best at the back of the border.

Even though there's a lot of fresh spring foliage now unfolding, don't forget that evergreens are invaluable for year-round interest and substance in the

PLANT OF THE MONTH

Clematis alpina
HEIGHT: 2.1 m (7 ft)
SPREAD: 1–1.5 m (3–5 ft)
FLOWERING TIME: April–May
POSITION: Sun or shade
SOIL: Any
HARDY?: Yes

The small-flowered clematis are much less demanding than their large-flowered cousins. A selection of species can give colour almost all the year round, though the fresh spring flowers and foliage of *Clematis alpina* take some beating. In late winter it starts to produce clusters of bright green leaves followed by beautiful nodding flowers. There are several varieties with blue, pink or white flowers, though blue ones like 'Frances Rivis' and 'Pamela Jackman' are the most attractive. This species isn't over-vigorous, so it can be grown even in the smallest space, supported on trellis or wires. For something a bit different, try growing it up a tripod in the border, or as a trailing plant to ramble down a bank or over a low wall.

The lime-green bracts of Euphorbia robbiae *are shown off beautifully against its evergreen rosettes of foliage. This tough, go-anywhere plant is happy in the sun or shade. In the background, pink peonies stand above a carpet of forget-me-nots.*

border, and they're best planted this month or in September. *Osmanthus* varieties are producing their creamy-white, exceptionally fragrant flowers this month. *O.* x *burkwoodii* and *O. delavayi* are two of the best varieties, which form rounded bushes of dark green, leathery leaves. One of the best evergreen climbers for a sheltered, south or west-facing wall is *Clematis armandii*, a vigorous plant bearing clusters of white or pink-flushed fragrant flowers that contrast well with its large, dark green leaves.

Winter-flowering heathers are finishing off for the season with a last flourish. Unlike a lot of other heathers, the many *E. carnea* varieties don't need a lime-free soil, and by choosing a succession of varieties you can have flowers from January to April. Those which are still flowering now include 'December Red' (rose-red flowers), 'Myretoun Ruby' (bright rose-pink), 'Ruby Glow' (dark red), and 'Foxhollow' (pale pink flowers and golden foliage).

Herbaceous perennials that started flowering last month are still going strong, and they're joined by the spurges (*Euphorbia*) with bold flower and foliage shapes that are ideal for providing structure in the garden. *E. robbiae* is invasive in good soil, though it's a handsome plant which is ideal for difficult places like dry shady sites under trees and hedges, and its evergreen rosettes of foliage look good in winter. *E. characias wulfenii* loves a dry sunny site and its tall flower heads are particularly handsome. *E. polychroma* makes a small rounded bush with bright yellow, flat heads of flowers.

Don't miss out on some of the old cottage-garden favourites. Lily-of-the-valley (*Convallaria*) has stems of white, strongly perfumed flowers. It grows well in shade, but be careful where you plant it because it spreads like wildfire. Candytuft (*Iberis sempervirens*) bears its heads of starched white flowers against dark green foliage, while *Alyssum saxatile* has bright yellow flowers that compliment and contrast with the colourful

cushions of blue, mauve or pink *Aubrieta*.

Welsh poppy (*Meconopsis cambrica*) bears lots of dainty, clear yellow flowers above clumps of fresh green foliage. Some people consider it to be a nuisance because it seeds itself all around the garden, but for all that it's a delightful thing to have. It grows just about anywhere, even in dense shade, and the yellow flowers look especially lovely with lime-green euphorbias.

Spring bedding is at its colourful best this month. Still real favourites are the good old wallflowers (*Cheiranthus*) which always look cheerful with their red or gold flowers. Interplant them with drifts of *Polyanthus* and forget-me-nots (*Myosotis*) with their many sprays of pale blue flowers and you'll have a real eye-catcher. But don't forget that they have to be sown in summer and planted in autumn. Forget-me-nots also self-seed easily, and they look lovely grown as informal masses under trees and shrubs.

Bulbs like daffodils are at their peak now and there are lots to choose from. They range from simple, yellow-flowering, single ones like 'Carlton' and whites such as 'Mount Hood' to double-flowered forms including 'Golden Ducat' and 'White Lion' and two-coloured ones like 'Passionale'. Tulips will be looking good too and there are dozens of different ones. The early double-flowered forms flower on 30 cm (1 ft) stems, so they're ideal for growing in containers; the taller Darwin hybrids are popular for bedding schemes; and the pretty dwarf *T. greigii* hybrids with unusual and attractive variegated leaves go well in tubs and the front of borders. If you haven't grown them, make a note to plant daffodils in August or early September and tulips up to November.

Many smaller bulbs also flower now, including the snake's-head fritillary (*Fritillaria meleagris*) with gorgeous, chequered, nodding flowers, and its stately cousin, the crown imperial (*F. imperialis*), which bears tall handsome flowers of gold, orange or red.

General tasks

Bindweed is a tenacious weed that can be hard to eradicate, especially in borders where it winds up plant stems. It can be killed with a systemic weedkiller like glyphosate, but don't get even a drop of chemical on your plants. Make its application easier by putting small bamboo canes next to the bindweed for it to climb up rather than up the plants, and when it's well established slip the mass of stems off the canes and soak them in weedkiller. Lay the treated bindweed on polythene so that your plants are protected and leave for several weeks for the weedkiller to take effect. It may take a couple of applications.

Containers and pots to be planted next month should be cleaned. Scrub out plastic hanging baskets and containers with hot water and household bleach. Clean terracotta and glazed pots using water and a stiff brush.

Scrubbing out used pots is one of the least appealing jobs, but it's vital to avoid any risk of disease or pests spreading to new, young plants.

Dead shrubs killed by hard frosts should be dug up and replaced, but make sure that they're definitely dead first. Using your thumbnail or a knife, scrape away a tiny patch of bark near the base: if it's green underneath, the plant is still alive and there's a good chance that it will regrow in the near future.

Grafted trees and shrubs should be inspected for shoots appearing on the stem beneath the knobbly graft. Rub them off when young, as they come from the rootstock and could eventually distort or dominate the plant.

Seeds should be stored carefully after opening. Most packets contain far more than is needed for one sowing, so keep the seed in good condition as it can last for years. Store packets of seed in a cool airy place or even in a sealed container in the refrigerator (but not the freezer). Damp, hot places are the worst possible conditions for seeds, so avoid kitchens and living rooms, and never keep them in the greenhouse.

See page 116 for details of harvesting and storing seed from the garden.

Shred prunings and stack them for six months to spread on the borders as a weed-suppressing mulch. Unless you have a large garden where it's worth buying a reasonably sized shredder, think about getting together with some neighbours to hire one for the weekend. There's lots of pruning done in spring, so now is the ideal time.

Slugs and snails are absolute pests at this time of year, so continue to protect plants as described on page 38. They feed at night, and it's often worth going out with a torch and collecting them up. Leaving a couple of planks on the ground encourages them to gather underneath, and the planks can be turned over in the morning to give birds a feast.

Ornamental garden

▶ *Deep-blue flowers of bugle (*Ajuga reptans) *stand out against the variegated grass* Holcus mollis *'Variegatus'. Ajuga spreads rapidly and can be increased by digging up the rooted stems.*

▼ *A coldframe is ideal for acclimatizing seedlings.*

ANNUALS AND BIENNIALS

Hardy annuals can still be sown outside. Plant out those you've raised under cover in a coldframe. If young plants have been grown in a heated greenhouse or on windowsills, slowly get them used to the colder conditions outside. Do this by putting them in a coldframe and gradually increasing the ventilation (or see this month's project, page 65).

Try to choose a few varieties that attract bees and butterflies, like alyssum, anchusa, candytuft, cornflower, godetia, larkspur and scabious. Bees are enormously useful in the garden, and butterflies are just as pretty as the flowers. In fact they were once described by an enthusiast as 'flying flowers'.

Ornamental grasses have delicate foliage and pretty flower heads that make an unusual contrast to other plants. They can be sown outside now.

Good annual varieties include quaking grass (*Briza maxima*) with nodding cone-shaped flower heads, squirrel-tail grass (*Hordeum jubatum*) which bears feathery ones, hare's-tail grass (*Lagurus ovatus*) with woolly flowers, and foxtail (*Setaria glauca*) with golden seed heads. The flower heads and seed heads of all varieties are excellent for arrangements.

Summer-flowering biennials like Canterbury bells and foxgloves should be transplanted to their flowering positions. Thin out foxgloves sown *in situ* to 30–45 cm (12–18 in) apart.

BULBS AND TUBERS

Dead-head larger bulbs like daffodils as soon as they finish flowering, so that they can put all their energy into building up their reserves for next year. Leave flower heads on smaller bulbs like snowdrops and scillas so that they can self-seed. During dry weather, water bulbs that have already flowered and feed with a tomato or rose fertilizer.

Summer-flowering bulbs and tubers such as 'poppy anemone' 'De Caen', wood hyacinth (*Galtonia candicans*), lilies, marvel of Peru (*Mirabilis jalapa*) and star of Bethlehem (*Ornithogalum*) should be planted by the end of the month. Blue African lily (*Agapanthus*) tubers can be planted now, but they often don't establish well: it's much better to buy pot-grown plants in a month or two.

Slugs adore newly emerged lily shoots and often chew through stems at ground level, so protect them as soon as the tips appear (see page 37).

◀ *Dahlias need staking, but put the stake in the hole before planting so you don't spear the tuber.*

▼ *If your soil is heavy, plant gladioli bulbs on a layer of coarse grit so they don't become waterlogged and rot.*

Dahlia tubers can be planted outside in warmer areas, but elsewhere delay planting until next month. They like a rich soil, so dig in plenty of organic matter and some slow-release fertilizer. Plant the tubers so that the tops or crowns are 7.5 cm (3 in) deep, and put in a stake *before* backfilling the planting hole as the tubers can easily be speared.

Tender bulbs, including gladioli, can now be planted out. They like a sunny sheltered site and well-drained soil. On heavy ground dig in coarse grit and put the bulbs on a layer of sand or grit so that they don't sit in water and rot. Gladioli can be grown in rows for cutting, in tubs, or planted in small groups in the border, 10 cm (4 in) apart and deep.

Other tender bulbs well worth growing include the 'peacock orchid' (*Acidanthera murielae*) which bears fragrant, white, purple-centred flowers in late summer, and *Nerine bowdenii* which produces stems of large pink flowers from mid to late autumn.

HERBACEOUS PERENNIALS AND ALPINES

Alpine troughs and containers are best planted now. The key to success with alpines is good drainage, so make sure that the containers have drainage holes and put a 5-cm (2-in)-thick layer of material like broken clay pots or gravel in the bottom. Then fill the container with compost made of equal parts of good garden soil, garden compost or finely chipped bark, and 3 mm (⅛ in) coarse grit. After planting spread a layer of grit over the surface which sets the plants off well, keeps their foliage dry and prevents them becoming splashed with soil.

Basal cuttings are a good way to increase many perennials when their new shoots are 7.5–10 cm (3–4 in) high. Gently scrape away a little soil around the crown of the plant and cut off several shoots as near to the base as possible, using a sharp knife. Put the cuttings into a pot of moist coir compost, cover with a polythene bag and stand in a warm, shady place or a coldframe until rooted. Irishman's cuttings are taken in a similar fashion but with a small amount of root attached, so they're almost certain to succeed.

Suitable plants that can be propagated by taking basal cuttings include *Achillea, Anthemis, Chrysanthemum, Delphinium, Euphorbia, Gypsophila,* lupins and mallows.

Finish dividing and replanting established clumps of perennials. Some late-flowering varieties prefer to be divided now rather than in autumn, including *Aster, Anthemis,* red-hot poker (*Kniphofia*), *Pyrethrum* (now *Tanacetum coccineum*) and Kaffir lily (*Schizostylis*).

Thin out densely growing clumps of perennials if they haven't been divided. Removing around a quarter to a third of weaker shoots gives remaining ones less competition, so they'll produce larger, better quality flowers.

LAWN
Roll new lawns sown last month to encourage growth from the base when the grass is about 5 cm (2 in) high. The roller on the back of a mower is usually adequate. A couple of days later cut the grass with the mower blades set at their highest level, gradually reducing the height of future cuts. Take care not to cut the grass too closely, especially in its first year.

Renovate an existing lawn at any time until autumn, though spring is best. To repair crumbled lawn edges, cut a square of turf to include the damaged part and turn it round 180 degrees so that the hole is in the body of the lawn. Top it up with soil and sow with grass seed.

Lumps are unattractive as they get scalped by the mower, so remove them by cutting and rolling back the turf, scraping away the soil underneath and replacing the grass in the same way as for treating hollows (right). Treat large hollows in a similar way, but also add soil. Fill small hollows by adding 2.5 cm (1 in)

REPAIRING A HOLLOW IN THE LAWN

Hollows in existing lawns are a nuisance because they allow coarse grasses to grow, which otherwise would be discouraged by regular cutting. However, they can be easily remedied without much disruption.

1 *To repair a hollow, first cut the turf with a spade or edging iron to create two 'flaps'.*

2 *Lift these flaps with the spade and roll them back. Fill the hollow with sifted garden soil.*

3 *Roll back the turf and tamp it down firmly using the back of a rake.*

▶ *Tulips may need to be planted annually if they're in a shady place, but they're extremely effective in the mixed border.*

of sifted garden soil and working it into the grass, though leave treating large areas in this way until autumn.

Clumps of coarse grass stand out like a sore thumb in an otherwise fine lawn. The best way to remove them is to simply criss-cross the clumps with an old kitchen knife and pull the grass out. Regular mowing is the best way to discourage coarse grasses.

Moss can be killed with chemicals, but this really treats only the symptom rather than the cause, which is poor drainage. Improve drainage by aerating (see page 15) and by raking out the layer of dead grass or 'thatch' that builds up at ground level and hinders drainage.

Continue weeding lawns and feed if you didn't last month. Trim the edges with a half-moon edging tool or a sharp spade to leave a clean edge for easy clipping with shears in future.

ROSES

Spray roses regularly with copper fungicide as a preventative measure against blackspot if they've suffered badly in previous years. If certain varieties are severely attacked every year, it's worth considering replacing them with ones that are naturally disease-resistant.

Plant clumps of chives under roses, as their roots exude a pungent white liquid that helps prevent blackspot after a couple of years. Their masses of mauve

April is a good month to take conifer cuttings. Fast-growing conifers like thujas, Leyland and Lawson's cypress can be grown easily from cuttings.

flower heads in summer are lovely too. Look out for the variety 'Forescate' which is more vigorous and has pink flowers.

Tie in shoots of climbers and ramblers regularly while they are still young and flexible to prevent wind damage. Pulling them downwards encourages flowering.

SHRUBS

Conifers can be propagated by cuttings. Pull off side shoots about 7.5–10 cm (3–4 in) long, trim the heel, dip the end in hormone rooting powder and put the cuttings into small pots of coir compost mixed with an equal quantity of grit. Put the pots in a shaded coldframe or a sheltered corner of the garden.

Deciduous shrubs with coloured foliage, like smoke tree (*Cotinus*), golden elder (*Sambucus racemosa* 'Plumosa Aurea') and *Spiraea x bumalda* varieties, benefit from pruning, which encourages plenty of bright new foliage. Cut back last year's growth by half, then feed to help intensify the leaf colours.

Evergreen hedges are best planted in spring. Shrubs are a much more versatile and ornamental alternative to a tall conifer hedge. They can be formally clipped, left to grow informally and to flower, and they can be dwarf or tall, depending on the plants you choose.

Taller plants that respond well to clipping include common holly (*Ilex aquifolium*) as well as many other attractively variegated hollies, golden privet (*Ligustrum ovalifolium* 'Aureum'), *Lonicera nitida* and its varieties 'Baggesen's Gold' and 'Silver Beauty'.

Dwarf clipped hedges are lovely for edging borders and herb gardens, including box (*Buxus sempervirens*), lavender, cotton lavender (*Santolina*) and wall germander (*Teucrium chamaedrys*).

Good informal hedging plants include *Berberis*, laurel (*Prunus laurocerasus* and *P. lusitanica*), firethorn (*Pyracantha*) and *Viburnum tinus*. In seaside areas, shrubs like *Escallonia*, *Olearia* and *Pittosporum* will tolerate salt-laden winds.

Forsythia can be pruned immediately after flowering, and large bushes of *F*. 'Lynwood' in particular need hard pruning to keep them under control. Cut all shoots back to within 5 cm (2 in) of last year's growth and remove around a third of the oldest, thickest branches at or near ground level to encourage new growth from the base.

Frost-damaged shoots on evergreens like Mexican orange blossom (*Choisya ternata)* should be pruned out. Cut back to healthy growth and take out any spindly weak shoots at the same time. Leave this job until next month in colder areas.

Lime-hating shrubs like rhododendrons and skimmias that are growing on neutral or limy soils commonly suffer from magnesium deficiency, which shows as yellow patches between green veins on the leaves. Water with a soluble fertilizer or make a more permanent change to the soil's acidity level by adding sulphur chips.

Silver-leaved shrubs like the curry plant (*Helichrysum serotinum*), lavender and cotton lavender (*Santolina*) should be pruned now. Cut straggly plants back to around 15 cm (6 in), otherwise just trim the bush lightly. Cutting plants hard back into old wood can be risky, so do it only if you've already rooted some cuttings last summer as insurance.

Wall-trained shrubs like the flowering quince (*Chaenomeles*) and *Forsythia suspensa* should be pruned immediately after flowering: cut back all outward-pointing shoots to within two or three buds of last year's growth. Other new shoots should be tied in, or pruned in the same way if the plant's beginning to outgrow its site.

Winter-flowering heathers should be lightly trimmed with shears after they have flowered.

All heathers can easily be propagated by layering. Select healthy stems on the outside of the plant and improve the soil underneath by mixing in a little compost and sand. Use a sharp knife to remove a small sliver of bark underneath where the stem will meet the soil. This wounding is not entirely necessary but it encourages roots to form. Peg the stem down firmly and cover it with soil where it meets the ground. Leave it for a year, by which time it should have rooted to form a new plant that can be detached and replanted.

Spreading varieties often layer themselves naturally, so it's worth prospecting around for ready-rooted stems.

WATER GARDEN
Aquatic plants are best planted in spring as the water is now warming up and they'll have a whole growing season to establish. Aquatics can be planted in special mesh containers. Older types with wide mesh need to be lined with hessian or woven plastic, though newer ones are made of finer mesh and don't need lining. Use sieved garden loam or special aquatic soil, *not* ordinary potting compost or soil which has been recently treated with chemicals or fertilizer. Place a little compost in the container, put the plant in so that its soil level is just below the rim, fill up with compost and firm gently. Top the container with fine gravel to stop the soil floating out, water it thoroughly and put it in the pond. Alternatively, if your pond has a layer of soil over the liner, simply push the roots into the mud.

Cleaning out established ponds is best done in spring, but don't do it too often or the water won't have a chance to reach a natural balance. As a rough guide, small ponds should be cleaned totally every five years, and large ponds every ten years. Clear a wildlife pond by dredging out debris rather than by emptying it and disturbing all the creatures.

Don't worry too much if your pond goes green at this time of year. The aquatic plants are only just coming into growth and they aren't yet vigorous enough to combat the algae, but they normally do so within a month or so.

Remove any blanketweed as it starts to grow, using a bamboo cane or a rake.

Established marginal plants and water lilies should be divided once they have formed large, overgrown clumps – normally after four to five years. Spread a large sheet of polythene beside the pond as a work-surface, and gather together all the materials needed so that the plants are out of the water for a short time only.

Divide marginals in the same way as herbaceous perennials (see page 37) by using an old knife or two garden forks back-to-back to split up the clump. Replant as described on page 64.

Water lilies consist of a rootstock with smaller side branches. Wash off the soil, remove the side shoots using a sharp knife and discard the old main stem. Dust the cut surfaces with sulphur to prevent infection and plant the side shoots as described on page 64.

Oxygenating plants should always be planted to help keep the water healthy. They take up surplus nutrients that otherwise provide food for green algae and blanketweed. In established ponds it's worth planting more oxygenators if algae are a regular problem. Water lilies are also useful, as their large leaves shade the water from too much sunlight which speeds algal growth.

To clean out a pond, first lift out the aquatic and marginal plants in containers and stand them in trays or buckets of water so they remain moist. Put fish, newts, clusters of spawn and tadpoles in containers of water. Bail out the pond water with a bucket or siphon it out with a hose, draining it into a lower part of the garden. It's best to put a net or strainer of some sort over the inlet so it doesn't become blocked with debris.

Once the pond is empty, scrub the inside with a stiff brush and clean water – don't use any detergents. Empty out the dirty dregs of water and refill it. Leave it to stand for a day or two so the temperature can stabilize before putting any fish back in the pond.

MAKE A COLDFRAME

Plants grown in the warmer, moister and windless conditions of the greenhouse or kitchen windowsill will need to be acclimatized to the colder temperatures outside. If you bring them straight out to biting winds and low night temperatures, they'll stop growing and could even fail completely.

Old hands will have a coldframe but newer gardeners might not and, like most capital items for the garden, they ain't cheap. So make yourself the great carrycot coldframe for no more than a couple of bob and half an hour's effort.

Get a large strong cardboard box from the supermarket or the electrical shop. Cut off the lid and paint the whole thing white inside and out. Then tape on a couple of string handles so that they go right underneath the box for support. The lid is a piece of clear rigid plastic held down with a brick or a bit of wood.

Using this you can conveniently bring your plants outside during the day and in again at night. Gradually open up the lid until it's open all day and then start leaving the box out at night, fully closed. Again, gradually open up until it's fully open day and night.

If you want a permanent outdoor coldframe there are lots of different, ready-made models on sale, though it's a lot cheaper to make your own. Use old floorboards to make a rectangular frame 120 cm (48 in) long and 60 cm (2 ft) wide. It should be about 33 cm (13 in) high at the back and sloping down to 28 cm (11 in) at the front. The top can be made from rigid plastic or glass edged with narrow timber, and hinged at the back so the lid can be easily opened.

Kitchen garden

FRUIT

Apples and pears should be inspected for pests and treated, if necessary, as described on (page 44). But never spray when the flowers are open or you'll kill the pollinating insects. The best time to spray is in the evening, when there are fewer beneficial insects around.

Black currants can be attacked by black currant gall mite (also called big bud mite) that causes the buds to swell and also spreads virus. Spray the plant with derris to kill the mites. There's no cure for the virus except the removal of affected buds, so it's as well to inspect your bushes on a regular basis.

Gooseberries can suffer from American gooseberry mildew, which appears as a white powdery coating on leaves and shoots. Grow resistant varieties like 'Invicta' and you'll never need to spray. Chemical gardeners spray with Nimrod T and repeat a fortnight later. Like all fungal diseases gooseberry mildew can often be prevented by keeping the plant in good health – pruning to let light and air through the bush, and adequate watering and feeding.

Prune fan-trained stone fruits like cherries, plums, peaches and nectarines by removing any shoots growing directly out from or into the wall. Thin out overcrowded or crossing shoots and remove any dead, diseased or damaged stems. Tie the remaining ones on to the framework of wires using garden twine or string.

Plums and cherries aren't pruned in winter as they're prone to attack by the fungal diseases silverleaf and bacterial

Fruit trees can be trained in various ways and even over arches to make a colourful and fruitful walkway. Trees for archways are best bought and planted as maidens (one-year-old trees), then trained as for cordons.

Asparagus is a delicious luxury vegetable which is quite easy to grow, though it does need to be planted in well-prepared soil.

canker, which get in through open wounds. Pruning when the tree is actively growing lets the cuts heal up quickly and lessens the risk of disease.

Bush cherries and plums are pruned in summer after fruiting.

Wall-trained fruit trees in flower such as apricots, pears and peaches should be protected from severe frosts with fleece, polythene or fine netting. Prepare the material in advance by stapling a 2.4–3-m (8–10-ft) length to a pole at either end, so that it can be quickly unrolled for easy protection when needed.

HERBS

Chives can be propagated by division. Large established clumps should be carefully lifted with a fork and divided into small clumps of bulbs for replanting.

Comfrey can be bought now and planted, in either groups or rows. The best form is Russian comfrey (*Symphytum* x *uplandicum*) though *S. officinale* is also good. Comfrey makes excellent ground cover, even on dry ground under trees, though it has a wealth of other uses. The leaves are rich in minerals, potash and nitrogen, and they can be harvested several times a year for use in several ways. Added to the compost heap, they make a good natural activator. They can be laid as a surface mulch around plants, particularly soft fruit or tomatoes that need lots

of potash, or they can be stored in a barrel and the resulting (pungent) liquid can be drained off, diluted at the rate of one part comfrey liquid to ten parts water and used as a liquid fertilizer.

It also has medicinal uses, as its common name of 'knitbone' shows: a poultice of comfrey leaves is said to speed healing not just of broken bones, but also of strains and bruises – ideal for the gardener, in fact! But be careful where you plant it. It can be *very* invasive.

Continue planting and sowing herbs as described on page 44. Thin March-sown seedlings to 15 cm (6 in) apart. Varieties that can also be sown outside now include balm, borage and summer savory. Sow parsley monthly to ensure a regular supply.

Thyme can be propagated by layering. Fill small pots with a 50/50 mix of coir compost and sharp sand, sink the pots in the ground underneath the vigorous outer shoots and peg the growths down firmly. In two or three months they will have rooted and the young plants can be removed and planted elsewhere.

Thymes are also best planted now, in a well-drained soil and a sunny site. They're ideal for pots – try several thymes with different foliage colours in a small terracotta strawberry pot with side and top planting holes.

VEGETABLES

Asparagus crowns can be bought and planted. Asparagus is expensive to buy as a vegetable, but it's economical to grow as it can crop for up to twenty years. Because the crop is long-lived, it really pays to prepare the site well in advance by digging in plenty of well-rotted manure. This is best done the previous autumn so it rots down thoroughly.

Buy one-year-old crowns, preferably an all-male variety such as 'Lucullus' or 'Franklim', and plant them as soon as possible, soaking the crowns in water for an hour before planting. Dig out a trench 15 cm (6 in) wide and deep for each row, with 30 cm (1 ft) between rows. Rake in a general fertilizer and shape the base of the trench to form a slight ridge in the middle. Put the crowns on the ridge 30 cm (1 ft) apart with their roots sloping down on each side, then backfill with soil at once – never leave the crowns exposed to dry out. Water in, and water well during dry weather.

Harvest established beds of asparagus from late April to early June. Don't harvest too much from young crops or the crowns will never be strong enough – pick a little in the second year, harvest over about four weeks in the third, and over about six weeks in subsequent years. Harvest the spears when they're 10–15 cm (4–6 in) long by cutting them cleanly with a sharp knife about 5 cm (2 in) below the ground. Never cut all the spears, but leave a few to leaf up and build the crown for next year.

Cabbages, cauliflowers and Brussels sprouts sown in a seedbed in March can be transplanted into their final positions and watered well after planting.

Make sure that you protect them right from the start against cabbage root fly. The little blighter is a common pest of all brassicas, not just cabbages. The adult flies lay their eggs in the soil around the plants, and the resulting small white grubs burrow into and eat the roots. The chemical Bromophos will give some protection, but the best form of prevention is to use collars. These fit snugly round newly transplanted seedlings and stop the flies laying their eggs. Collars can be bought, or you can make your own by cutting 15-cm (6-in) squares of foam rubber carpet underlay with a slit on one side to the centre. They must fit really tightly around the stem to be effective.

Blanching celery sown under cover should be planted out into prepared trenches. Dig out a trench 30 cm (12 in) deep and 38 cm (15 in) wide. Fork in well-rotted manure and refill with soil to within 10 cm (4 in) of the top. Leave the rest of the trench open. Self-blanching types don't need trenching. Plant them 25 cm (10 in) apart each way.

Dwarf French beans can be sown under cloches in mild areas, but remember to put the cloches out several weeks before sowing to warm the soil. Sow two seeds per station 20 cm (8 in) apart with 30 cm (1 ft) between rows, and thin to one seedling per station.

In colder areas sow under glass (see page 72) or wait until next month.

Flea beetle attacks cabbages, turnips and radish, making many tiny holes in the leaves. Dust with derris powder as soon as the first signs are seen.

Peas sown earlier will need support, either from twiggy pea sticks or netting supported by canes.

Maincrop potatoes set out to sprout last month must be planted by the middle of the month. Space them 38 cm (15 in) apart with 75 cm (2½ ft) between rows. Once the foliage shows through, be prepared to protect from frost with fleece or by earthing up (see page 45).

Seakale is an unusual perennial vegetable that can be blanched indoors or

Putting collars around brassica plants is a safe, organic and completely effective way to protect them against cabbage root fly.

Spacing of Vegetables Sown Outside

Type	Spacing between plants when thinned	Spacing between rows
Beetroot	7.5 cm (3 in)	30 cm (1 ft)
Carrot	7.5 cm (3 in)	30 cm (1 ft)
Chinese Cabbage	23 cm (9 in)	23 cm (9 in)
Kale	45 cm (1½ ft)	45 cm (1½ ft)
Kohl Rabi	23 cm (9 in)	30 cm (1 ft)
Lettuce	23 cm (9 in)	30 cm (1 ft)
Parsnip	15 cm (6 in)	30 cm (1 ft)
Peas	5 cm (2 in)	45 cm (1½ ft)
Salad Onion	Sow thinly	7.5 cm (3 in)
Salad Rocket	7.5 cm (3 in)	30 cm (1 ft)
Salsify	Sow thinly	15 cm (6 in)
Scorzonera	15 cm (6 in)	30 cm (1 ft)
Spinach	15 cm (6 in)	30 cm (1 ft)
Swiss Chard	30 cm (1 ft)	35 cm (15 in)
Spinach Beet	30 cm (1 ft)	30 cm (1 ft)

outside to harvest in winter and early spring. Rooted cutting or 'thongs' can be bought and planted now. Seakale likes a well-drained soil that has had plenty of well-rotted manure added the previous winter, and an open sunny site.

Rub off all but the strongest bud from the thongs and plant 5 cm (2 in) deep and 38 cm (15 in) apart.

Thin out vegetables sown earlier in rows to the spacings given in the table (vegetables sown in modules and planted out won't need thinning). These spacings are optimum ones, which is fine if you've got plenty of room, but you can often get away with smaller spacings. If you decide on the latter course, it's important that the plants have plenty of food and water to reduce competition, and crops should be harvested as soon as they begin to mature.

Sow vegetables outside. All those listed in the table may now be sown directly into the ground. Follow the table for the correct spacing between rows. Salad crops in particular should be sown little and often to provide a regular supply while avoiding a glut.

Florence fennel can now be sown in milder areas, in rows 45 cm (1½ ft) apart. In colder areas delay until next month or sow under cover.

Sow leeks, Brussels sprouts, cabbage and broccoli in short rows 15 cm (6 in) apart in a seedbed.

Vegetables sown in modules last month can be planted out under cloches. For spacings see page 46.

There's a wide range of cloches available to suit every budget. They create an ideal protected environment for bringing on vegetable crops early, as well as strawberries and flowers. Ready-made cloches are usually available in glass, rigid plastic or polycarbonate, and flexible plastic. If you have a cheap source of glass or rigid plastic, it may be a better option to make your own 'tent-shaped' cloches by using special cloche clips to fix the panes together at the top.

Greenhouse and windowsill

Annual climbers can be sown early this month. They're tremendously useful plants that suit lots of different situations. Grow them through established shrubs, conifers and other climbers for extra summer colour, up tripods or supports in containers or borders, or just up walls and fences. All these annual climbers should be planted out in late May or early June after all danger of frost is past.

Chickabiddy (*Asarina scandens*) produces many blue, pink or white trumpet-shaped flowers. *A. barclaiana* 'Angel's Trumpet' bears large, bright pink trumpets or flowers. Sow two seeds per 7.5-cm (3-in) pot at 21°C (70°F). Thin to one seedling.

Cup-and-saucer plant (*Cobaea scandens*) produces purple bell-shaped flowers with a basal 'ruff' from mid-summer onwards. There's also a choice form called 'Alba' with pure white flowers.

Morning glory (*Ipomoea tricolor* 'Heavenly Blue') has exquisite, large, blue flowers. Soak the seeds overnight and sow as above. A new variety *I. hirsuta* 'Mini Sky-Blue', is said to be more compact and free-flowering and ideal for containers. Moon flower (*I. alba*) has huge white saucers of flowers that open in the evening to give off a delicious scent.

Canary creeper (*Tropaeolum peregrinum*) bears many bright yellow, fringed flowers all along its long stems. This vigorous plant is easy to grow – sow two seeds per pot indoors in late April, and thin to one seedling. Alternatively sow the seed outdoors in May.

Chilean glory vine (*Eccremocarpus scaber*) is a quick-growing perennial climber that can be treated like an annual (see page 48). The same applies to the purple bell vine (*Rhodochiton atrosanguineum*) with its unusual, dark purple, almost black flowers.

Basil is an indispensable herb that should be sown now. Sow seeds thinly in a tray and prick out into 7.5-cm (3-in) pots when large enough to handle. Young plants should be planted out only when all danger of frost is past.

Cyclamen that have flowered should be given decreasing amounts of water as the foliage turns yellow and dies back. Remove the dead leaves to prevent the corm rotting. Once all the foliage has died back, put the pot on its side under the greenhouse staging or in a shed to 'rest' for the summer.

Amaryllis (*Hippeastrum*) bulbs should be put to rest in the same way.

Hanging baskets can be planted up and grown on under cover if there's enough space, so they'll be well established by the time they go outside at the end of May when all danger of frost should be past. See page 71 for planting details.

Seedlings are now growing strongly and need regular watering, especially on sunny days.

Harden off young vegetables, rooted cuttings and annuals before planting out, otherwise they'll be severely checked. A coldframe is ideal for hardening off – leave the lid open during the day and close it at night for a week, then leave it half-open for another week (or see this month's project on page 65). If frost is forecast, cover the frame with bubble polythene for extra protection.

Meconopsis betonicifolia, the beautiful Himalayan blue poppy, can be grown from seed, though it does need special treatment. Sow the seed thinly on a pot of coir compost and keep at 21°C (70°F) for two weeks. Move to a shelf in the refrigerator (put the pot in a polythene bag for the sake of hygiene!) and the seedlings should begin to appear in a fortnight or so. At this point, move it back into a warm position.

Shading, watering and ventilation should all be carefully monitored. April can bring anything from blazing sunshine to long periods of rain, so look after your plants accordingly. Strong sunshine will scorch the delicate leaves of young cuttings and seedlings, therefore shade the greenhouse if necessary by applying a thin coat of shading paint, which is rather like whitewash. Alternatively lay sheets of newspaper over seedlings temporarily.

Damp down the greenhouse on hot days by spraying paths with water to keep the atmosphere humid.

Shrubs can be raised from seed sown in spring. Not only is it fascinating to grow something different from seed, but you can also save a fair bit of money if you have a large garden to plant.

Sow seed thinly in pots of coir compost mixed with a little vermiculite, and cover very lightly with the same material. Put the pots in the greenhouse or on a windowsill in gentle heat, and transplant the seedlings individually into small pots when they're large enough to handle. Some plants take a while to germinate, so be patient.

Shrubs to sow now include *Abutilon vitifolium*, butterfly bush (*Buddleia*), parrot's bill or lobster's claw (*Clianthus*), honeysuckle (*Lonicera*), tree lupin (*Lupinus arboreus*), Russian sage (*Perovskia*) and Cape figwort (*Phygelius*).

Several varieties need a little special treatment. Put *Cytisus* and *Genista* seeds in boiling water and leave them to soak overnight to soften their hard seed coats.

Eucalyptus species are easy and quick to grow, given a period of cold first. Put the seeds in a little damp sand in a polythene bag, and put it in the refrigerator for several weeks first.

Cape primrose (*Streptocarpus*) can be propagated by leaf cuttings. Pull a complete, fully grown leaf off a healthy plant,

---

VEGETABLES TO GROW UNDER COVER

In modules

Sow dwarf French beans two seeds per cell and thin to one seedling. Sow climbing French beans one seed per cell, Florence fennel two seeds per cell and thinned to one seedling, and leeks six seeds per cell, but left unthinned.

Sow runner beans one seed per cell, provided you're in a mild area where they can be planted out around mid-May. Otherwise delay sowing until late April/early May. Runner beans are fast-growing and their growth will be checked if they have to sit around in pots.

In trays

Celery and celeriac can be sown thinly in trays and covered with a little vermiculite, at a temperature of 18°C (65°F). Prick out seedlings into trays when they're large enough to handle.

In pots

Marrows, courgettes, pumpkins and squashes can be sown now at a temperature of around 18°C (65°F). Sow two seeds per 7.5-cm (3-in) pot, placing the seeds on their sides, and thin to one seedling.

They take up a lot of space in the garden, but trailing varieties can be grown up arches or other supports. Not only do they look great but the fruits are also much less likely to be nibbled by slugs.

Sweetcorn can be sown at a temperature of 18–21°C (65–70°F). Sow two seeds per 7.5-cm (3-in) pot, and thin to leave one seedling.

cut it into 2.5-cm (1-in) sections and stand the pieces on end and the 'right' way up, just burying the base, in a small pot of coir compost mixed 50/50 with vermiculite. Note that the part of the leaf which was nearest the plant should be downwards. Put the pots in a warm shady place and small plantlets should develop from the bottom of the leaf sections in a couple of months.

A similar method which produces more plants is to cut the adult leaf in half down the middle of the central vein, and put the two pieces on their sides on to trays of compost. Several plantlets should grow on the edge.

African violets (*Saintpaulia*) can also be propagated by leaf cuttings, this time using the complete leaf plus a piece of the leaf stem.

Take cuttings from tender perennials, dahlias and chrysanthemums as described on pages 28 and 133. To encourage bushy growth, pinch out the tops of cuttings rooted last month which are growing strongly – unless they are to be trained as standards. (See page 125 for how to train standards.) Cuttings taken earlier which are well rooted should be potted up into the next size of pot.

Continue to buy and pot up young plants or 'plugs' which can be bought from garden centres.

Continue to sow aubergines, cucumbers and tomatoes as described on page 48. Pot up plants sown earlier.

Pot up peppers into the next largest pot as soon as they have fully rooted round their present pot. When they're full of root they can go into their final 23-cm (9-in) pots.

Plant out aubergines, tomatoes and okra into peat-free growing bags, large pots or the greenhouse border. Stake the plants and give them plenty of light, or they'll develop long weak shoots.

Vine weevil is a real vandal in the greenhouse. The creamy-white grubs live in the soil and feed at night, so they often go unnoticed until the colony is well established. Set up an 'early-warning system' by putting a few 'gourmet' vine weevil plants such as primulas and strawberries around the greenhouse, in pots which can be regularly inspected. Once discovered, vine weevils can be effectively controlled with a biological predator. It's a microscopic worm that attacks the grub. You buy it as a powder, mix it with water and simply water it on. Standing the feet of greenhouse staging in bowls of water stops the flightless adult beetles climbing up the legs.

Winter-flowering pansies are best sown now in gentle heat. Sow the seed thinly in trays, cover with a very shallow layer of compost and then a sheet of black polythene to exclude the light. Transplant them when the seedlings are large enough to handle. They flower from autumn right through to spring, unless the winter weather is severe.

CHECKLIST

- Before hoeing borders, look for self-sown seedlings of plants, which could be potted up and grown on.
- Continue weeding. A short 'onion' hoe is useful for close weeding between young plants and seedlings.
- Feed established roses with rose fertilizer.
- Dig up perennial weeds as soon as they appear.
- Prepare trenches for runner beans and sweet peas if you didn't do this earlier (see page 22).
- Protect newly planted evergreens with windbreaks of polythene or netting in exposed sites.
- Remember to harvest forced rhubarb.
- Continue staking tall varieties of perennials.
- Hang yellow sticky traps in the greenhouse to catch pests.
- Tie in clematis regularly as they can quickly form a tangled mass of shoots.
- Water new plants during dry weather.
- Remove mulches used to protect tender plants over winter.

MAY

I N MAY THE WEATHER can be all over the place. Newer gardeners are likely to be lulled into a false sense of security early in the month if the weather's warm. It often is, but then it can cruelly change to deliver frosts later on. Old hands, therefore, will wait to plant tender plants until the first week in June.

However, you should be able to harvest piles of vegetables from under your cloches, to say nothing of plate after plate of delicious asparagus. You'll be able to guarantee that the borders will be bursting with flowers and fresh new foliage, the birds will be filling your garden with music and the first real buzz of insect life will remind you that summer isn't far away. Ah, it's a good life at this time of year!

◀ *The golden rain tree (*Laburnum*) drips with flowers in May and June. Here it's trained over an arch with wisteria. The purple blooms of ornamental onions (*Allium*) make a lovely colour contrast.*

GARDENS TO VISIT

- **Bodnant Garden**, Gwynedd, North Wales. Formal Italianate terraces a vast lily pond, and woodland plants. Masses of spring colour from bulbs and shrubs. Famous laburnum arch looks best in early summer. Spectacular autumn colour. Restaurant, plants for sale.
- **Branklyn**, Tayside. Unusual and exquisite acid-loving plants including dwarf rhododendrons. Extensive collection of alpines looks best in spring. *Meconopsis* in early summer. Wonderful autumn colour. Plants for sale.
- **Chelsea Physic Garden**, London SW3. A must for anyone interested in herbs and garden history. Range of herbs grouped by uses. Scented plants. Many unusual varieties.
- **Sissinghurst**, Kent. Created by Vita Sackville-West. Much of it is divided into small areas, including a cottage garden, herb garden, roses, and white garden. Very popular, so check before you visit. Shop and restaurant.

Looking good

May brings an exuberance of flower. Many trees and shrubs are almost bowed down under the weight of their blossoms, and herbaceous perennials are shooting out of the ground so quickly that you can almost watch them grow. As well as all the flowers, the subtle tints of fresh young foliage make up a marvellous tapestry of colour.

Flowering trees are making a wonderful display of blossom. There are many flowering cherries (*Prunus*) including the Lombardy cherry ('Amanogawa'), popular for small spaces as it forms a narrow upright column of branches clothed with double, pale pink flowers. By contrast 'Shirofugen' develops into a wide-spreading tree laden with double white flowers.

Ornamental thorn trees (*Crataegus laevigata*) can be even more showy than flowering cherries. 'Paul's Scarlet' bears double scarlet flowers, 'Crimson Cloud' has single dark red ones with a pretty white eye, and 'Rosea Flore Pleno' has double pink blossoms. There are some attractive, more subtle varieties too, like *C.l.* 'Plena' which has double, white flowers. *C. prunifolia* looks handsome from spring to autumn, with white flowers, long-lasting red fruits and gleaming oval leaves that colour beautifully in autumn. And don't shun the white-flowered common hawthorn (*C. monogyna*) which makes an excellent prickly hedge that's a wonderful wildlife habitat. Grow a wild rose through it and you have the best of all rural worlds.

The flower colours of crab apples (*Malus*) tend to be more subtle. Those varieties which started flowering last month are still going strong, and they're now joined by later ones like *M. coronaria* 'Charlottae' which bears double, pink, scented flowers. 'Profusion' has dark red flowers, and 'John Downie' bears white ones (this is also the best culinary variety). There are many other varieties available. Both thorns and crab apples are particularly good because, as well as spring flowers, they'll also have lots of colourful fruits in autumn. That's just the sort of double value you need if your garden's small.

For a total colour contrast, the golden rain tree (*Laburnum*) positively drips with long clusters of bright yellow flowers. At Bodnant and Barnsley House there are stunning pathways of *Laburnums*. Do bear in mind, though, that all parts of this tree are poisonous, particularly the seeds, so it's wise not to plant laburnums if there are young children around. Never plant one near a pond as the seeds will poison the water.

Several choice, less usual trees are also flowering now. The Judas tree (*Cercis siliquastrum*) bears many dangling clusters of rosy-pink flowers just before the attractive rounded leaves appear. It's said to be the tree from which Judas hanged himself, hence its name. Another excellent small tree is the rose acacia (*Robinia hispida*) which also bears deep rose-pink flowers and has pretty, fern-like leaves. Both these trees like a sheltered sunny site. The snowbell tree (*Styrax japonica*) has wide-spreading branches and its exquisite, small, white flowers hang from underneath. Also known as the snowbell or snowdrop tree, *Halesia carolina* bears similar beautiful white flowers. Both the snowbell trees need a moist, lime-free soil.

Paulownia tomentosa gives a glorious display of deep mauve, foxglove-like flowers in May, provided the weather has been kind, and its large velvety leaves look exceptionally handsome. It forms a round-headed tree about 10 m (33 ft) high. Alternatively, if you want some dramatic foliage without the flowers, prune it to the ground in spring and then remove all but one of the new shoots. This remaining one will grow to around 3 m (10 ft) in one season and will be clothed with huge leaves.

Shrubs in flower include many white ones this month. One of the loveliest is *Exochorda* x *macrantha* 'The Bride', with arching branches smothered in clusters of large, pure white flowers. The poetically named bridal wreath or foam of May (*Spiraea* 'Arguta') also bears masses of white flowers. For a combination of attractive flowers and all-year foliage, there's little to beat Mexican orange blossom (*Choisya ternata*) which bears fragrant white flowers in bursts through late spring and summer, and its attractive evergreen foliage looks good all year. 'Aztec Pearl' is a compact variety. *C.t.* 'Sundance' has pale gold leaves, though the flowers aren't produced nearly so freely.

Nearly everyone falls in love with the beautiful waxy-petalled blooms of magnolias, though remember that as most varieties develop into large shrubs, they'll need plenty of room. The most compact species is *M. stellata* which grows to around 2.4 m (8 ft), with flowers that are a mass of narrow petals. *M.* x *soulangeana* bears huge tulip-shaped blooms. Most varieties have white flowers, but those of 'Lennei' are flushed with red and 'Rustica Rubra' has rich purple-red flowers. There are many other beautiful and less common magnolias, like *M. sieboldii*, which should be planted with a view to the longer term as they can take a few years to flower. Some species need to be grown on an acid soil, so check them out first.

Spring just wouldn't be the same without the scent of lilacs. The vast majority are varieties of *Syringa vulgaris* which grow into large shrubs. There are lots of colours from which to choose including 'Madame Lemoine' (white), 'Firmament' (sky-blue), 'Katherine Havemeyer' (deep lavender-purple), 'Edward J. Gardner' (pale pink), 'Sensation' (purple-red edged with white) and 'Primrose' (pale yellow). For a small space, choose the more compact variety *S. meyeri* 'Palibin' with pale pink flowers.

Daphnes are just about the only plants that can beat lilacs for spring fragrance. These choice plants are a bit pricey, but

THE GARDEN INDOORS

FLOWERS FOR FOOD

Flowers make lovely table decorations, but they're not only good to look at. They can be used to add colour and flavour to a whole range of dishes.

Crystallized flowers like rose petals, primroses and violets add a delightful touch to iced cakes, trifles and other sweet dishes. Wash the flowers and leave them to dry, then brush them with egg white and dust with fine sugar. Let the flowers dry for several hours before using them.

Nasturtiums (*Tropaeolum majus*) are perfect for livening up salads with their brightly coloured flowers. Their leaves and seeds have a peppery flavour and they're a good salad ingredient, as are the flower buds of day lily (*Hemerocallis*), if you can bear to cut them. Borage (*Borago officinalis*) has pretty blue flowers that can also be used to decorate salads, or they can be floated on cool summer drinks.

Marrows and courgettes produce large yellow flowers (above) that have actually become a gourmet dish at top restaurants. Pick the flowers just before they're fully open, shake them to remove any insects inside and wash them thoroughly. They're delicious coated in batter and deep-fried. Serve them as an unusual side dish.

A few words of caution, however. Use only recommended plants, and make certain that you have the correct varieties before eating them. Never eat any plants that have recently been sprayed with chemicals.

their perfume is second to none. *Daphne burkwoodii* bears pale pink flowers, and the variety 'Astrid' has pretty green and white variegated leaves. There are also dwarf varieties for rockeries like *D. collina* and *D.* x *napolitana*.

Rhododendron varieties are at their peak now. About the best types for containers are the *Rhododendron yakushimanum* hybrids. This relatively new group includes many plants with delicate and unusually coloured flowers like 'Doc', which has rose-pink blooms with deeper pink edges, fading to white as they age; those of 'Percy Wiseman' are cream flushed with pink; 'Hoppy' is pale mauve fading to white; 'Silver Sixpence' has creamy-white flowers splashed with pale yellow. Although they grow only to around 1 m (3 ft), their leaves are much larger and more attractive than those of other dwarfs.

Climbers really begin to flower in earnest this month, clothing walls, fences and pergolas with curtains of colour. There are so many different clematis that a carefully chosen range of varieties can give colour from early spring to late autumn. One of the easiest species to grow is *Clematis montana* with masses of white flowers. 'Rubens' and 'Elizabeth' are pale pink. All these are rampant and they can easily grow up to 6 m (20 ft), so give them plenty of space. Less vigorous ones which are easier to accommodate are *C. alpina* and *C. macropetala* varieties, with pretty, nodding, blue or pink flowers and ferny, fresh green foliage.

Large-flowered hybrid clematis are a little more choosy in their requirements. They need a soil rich in organic matter and nutrients, and they prefer to have their roots in the shade and their heads in the sun. Because they reach only about 1.8–2.4 m (6–8 ft), they can be grown in lots of different places – over arches, pergolas and arbours, up walls and fences, or even up free-standing posts or supports to give rapid height to a border. Even better, because their slender, twining stems don't strangle other plants, they can be grown through trees, shrubs,

Spring-flowering clematis species like this Clematis montana 'Elizabeth' are easy to grow and reliable. The sumptuous velvety purple Iris germanica flowers make a wonderful display.

combined with other climbing plants, and even draped over ground-cover plants like heathers, to give an extra burst of summer colour. In a small garden, clematis are really invaluable. Do bear in mind, though, that only the large-flowered hybrids and the less vigorous clematis species can be combined with other plants in this way. Rampant species like *C. montana* would quickly overwhelm another plant.

There are many gorgeous hybrids flowering now. 'Nelly Moser' is an old favourite with pink-and-white striped flowers. 'Bee's Jubilee' and 'Capitaine Thuilleaux' have similar blooms. There are some lovely blues, including 'Beauty of Worcester' (double, deep blue), 'Lasurstern' (lavender blue), 'H.F. Young' (Wedgwood blue) and 'Mrs Cholmondeley' (pale blue). Varieties with bright, vibrant-coloured flowers include 'Fireworks' (bluish-purple with a dark red bar), 'Dr Ruppel' (rose-red with a brighter pink bar) and 'Barbara Jackman' (mauve with a crimson bar and pale stamens).

Wisteria makes a truly breathtaking show of flowers in May and June. This plant takes a few years to produce a really good display, but it's definitely worth the wait as the long showers of scented flowers falling from a wall or pergola look absolutely magnificent. There are white- and pink-flowering wisterias, but the blue varieties are by far the best. Always buy plants that have been produced by grafting as they'll usually flower within a couple of years, whereas those produced by other methods can take five years or more. You should be able to see the graft right at the base of the plant. Encourage shy-flowering wisterias to bloom by feeding with a high-potash fertilizer in late winter or early spring.

Water-garden plants are now beginning to flourish. Brightest of all is the kingcup or marsh marigold (*Caltha palustris*) which often starts producing its beautiful, bright gold blooms in April. There is a double-flowered form with yellow 'pompon' flowers, and the giant of the family is *C. polypetala*, which can grow up to 1 m (3 ft) high and wide. Kingcups contrast perfectly with the pretty blue flowers of the water forget-me-not (*Myosotis scorpioides*).

Bog bean (*Menyanthes trifoliata*) is a useful plant for concealing pond edges with its thick, scrambling stems, and it bears prettily fringed, white or pink-tinged flowers on short stems. The vertical foliage of grasses and rushes make a striking contrast. Those with variegated leaves look attractive all season, like *Acorus calamus* 'Variegatus' with iris-like leaves boldly striped with cream and green, and *Glyceria maxima variegata* with narrow green and white leaves that are flushed with pink in spring. This plant is invasive, so it's best to grow it in a container either in the pond or bog garden.

In the bog garden, globe flowers (*Trollius*) bear many rounded heads of yellow or orange flowers on stems above their attractive divided leaves. Water avens (*Geum rivale*) produces nodding heads of coppery-orange flowers. No bog garden is complete without a few candelabra primulas with their attractive orange, red or yellow flowers, like *Primula helodoxa*, *P. bulleyana*, *P. pulverulenta* and *P. japonica*. One of the most handsome varieties is the giant Himalayan cowslip (*P. florindae*) with delicately scented heads of yellow flowers borne on tall stems 60-90 cm (2-3 ft) high. *P. sikkimensis* has a similar appearance but is more compact. *P. vialii* is slightly later flowering, but this tiny primula is a real gem. Its poker-shaped flowers are purple tipped with red, and they look almost orchid-like.

For the larger bog garden, *Peltiphyllum peltatum* is a handsome plant. The stems of waxy pink flower-clusters appear alone, to be followed in early summer by large, rounded, bronze-green leaves. If you've got loads of space, the giant rhubarb *Gunnera manicata* makes a real talking-point, with massive leaves that can be up to 1 m (3 ft) across on stems 1.8 m (6 ft) high. A compact alternative is *Rodgersia*, with handsome, large, lobed leaves and feathery plumes of flowers.

General tasks

Garden pests need to be carefully monitored. Using chemicals to control garden pests and diseases may be necessary in severe cases, but widespread use of chemicals often makes things worse in the long term as they kill both the pest *and* its natural predators like ladybirds and hoverfly larvae. If you have to spray, do it as late as possible in the evening when there are fewer beneficial insects around, and on a wind-less day.

Prevention is much better than cure. Healthy plants are far more resistant to attack, just like humans, so it really does pay to keep the soil, and therefore the plants growing in it, in good heart. Prepare the ground well before planting by adding plenty of compost or well-rotted manure and some organic fertilizer. Water plants during dry spells and top up the feeding with a liquid fertilizer to keep them growing strongly. The old maxim of getting out of the soil only what you put in really does hold true.

Attracting wildlife also pays dividends because birds, hedgehogs, ladybirds, ground beetles and a host of others will consume large quantities of insect pests. Encourage these creatures by providing water and somewhere to live. There's lots of natural shelter in mixed plantings of trees, shrubs, perennials and other plants, and it also helps to leave a few piles of leaves or twigs around, especially in autumn and winter.

Encourage birds like tits and even nuthatches by providing nest boxes. Take care when you're siting nestboxes, as you could be providing an easy meal for bird predators. The boxes should be at least 1.8 m (6 ft) off the ground, on a wall, fence or tree trunk that isn't easily climbed by cats. Protect the boxes from cats by surrounding nestboxes on tree trunks with a 'collar' of prickly prunings, both above and below the box. If there are lots of magpies in your area, surround the nestbox with 5-cm (2-in) wire netting, which lets small birds through but stops larger ones from robbing the nest. Natural nest sites are often best, so plant plenty of prickly shrubs and hedges to create dense cover for smaller birds. With so many natural pest controllers in your garden, you shouldn't need to spray at all.

Bare soil is best hoed regularly to keep down weeds as they germinate. It's far easier to get them at this stage rather than when they've become established or, even worse, seeded everywhere so you have hundreds more next year. Use a small onion hoe to weed closely around plants.

Water shrubs, trees and other plants that were put out in autumn or spring. A few days of sunny weather accompanied by a brisk wind will soon dry out the ground. In such cases, plants may need daily watering.

Birds are excellent pest controllers. They'll eat greenfly, caterpillars and lots of other unwanted visitors particularly when they have nests full of hungry fledglings to feed. Even a small bird can eat hundreds of insects in one day.

Ornamental garden

ANNUALS, BIENNIALS AND TENDER PERENNIALS

Biennials should be sown now to flower next spring and early summer. Sow the seed outside in a well-prepared seedbed and transplant the seedlings 15 cm (6 in) apart once they're large enough to handle.

Popular biennials include wallflower (*Cheiranthus cheiri*), sweet William (*Dianthus barbatus*), foxglove (*Digitalis*), sweet rocket or dame's violet (*Hesperis matronalis*), honesty (*Lunaria annua*) and forget-me-not (*Myosotis*).

Forget-me-nots that have finished flowering can be left to set seed, unless the ground has to be cleared for summer bedding. When the seed is brown and ripe, either collect it for sowing elsewhere or scatter it by shaking the dying plants when they're pulled up.

Dig up and compost biennials that have been used for spring bedding to make way for summer-flowering plants. Revitalize the ground by digging in some well-rotted compost or manure and a little organic fertilizer.

Border chrysanthemums can be planted out, spaced 30 cm (1 ft) apart. To grow chrysanthemums for cutting, plant them in double rows with 23 cm (9 in) between plants. Support them individually with canes or, if you grow a lot, use strong wire mesh with 23 cm (9 in) squares. Tie each corner to 1 m (3 ft) wooden posts and gradually raise the mesh as the plants grow.

Containers can be planted up with frost-tender plants at the end of the month. They'll make a really stunning display right through the summer and, though they need regular attention they're not difficult.

Half-hardy annuals raised under cover can be planted out at the end of the month in milder districts, provided they've been hardened off first (see page 65). In colder areas or if late frosts are forecast, delay planting until next month and give the plants a liquid feed to keep them growing strongly. It's far better to put them out a couple of weeks later, when they can grow on steadily, than have them checked by a late frost.

Hardy annuals sown earlier should be thinned to leave about 10 cm (4 in) between plants. Water them well an hour or so beforehand, which reduces root disturbance. The thinnings can be used to fill gaps elsewhere. Lift the seedlings carefully with a trowel, handle them by the leaves to avoid bruising the stems, and water them well after replanting.

Seed can still be sown outside, though it's best to complete any sowing by the end of the month.

CONTAINER PLANTS FOR SUMMER COLOUR

The best plants for masses of summer flowers are half-hardy annuals and tender perennials. You can raise your own plants from seeds and cuttings in a greenhouse or on a sunny windowsill, or you can buy young plants in early spring for potting and growing on. Of course, there are plenty of ready-grown plants on sale now, but don't buy them before the end of the month unless they're staying under cover, or you could lose them to a late frost.

There's an enormous range of plants from which to choose. Old favourites like begonias, geraniums, fuchsias, petunias and lobelia can be combined for a mass of colour. It's down to individual taste whether you prefer flaming colours or subtle shades. Keep a look out for new versions of old faithfuls, like double-flowered busy Lizzies (*Impatiens*) and the 'New Guinea hybrids' with attractive foliage. 'Surfina' petunias are fast-growing and produce masses of flowers in many colours, including white, pale pink, dark pink and purple. There are new fuchsias like the 'Fantasia' varieties with upright-facing flowers, and *F. triphylla* 'Thalia' is fast becoming a real favourite with its purple-red leaves and clear red blooms. See page 101 for trailing plants for the edges of containers.

Sweet peas growing in rows for cutting should be loosely tied to their supports with soft string. Pinch off side shoots and tendrils as they appear. Feed all sweet peas weekly with a liquid fertilizer and water them well during dry spells.

Tender perennials that have been over-wintered under cover can also be hardened off and planted out at the end of the month. Putting out young plants raised from cuttings in autumn or spring should be delayed until June.

Tender perennials are ideal for borders and containers as they flower for months on end, often right through autumn, though they do need a sunny site to perform really well. See page 128 for a description of varieties.

If you're buying new plants from garden centres, be careful of those with lots of very fresh, soft, young growth. They may have just come out of a greenhouse and they'll need to be hardened off for a couple of weeks before planting. If in doubt, don't buy them until next month.

Frost-tender plants are ideal for containers as they flower for months on end. Those growing under cover can be moved outside towards the end of the month.

83

Bulbs and Tubers

Pests and diseases can sometimes be a problem, though bulbs are normally trouble-free provided they're not growing in unsuitable conditions. Infected bulbs should be dug up and burnt or put in the dustbin – not on the compost heap.

Eelworm causes distorted yellowing leaves. Cut open affected bulbs to reveal tell-tale brown rings. Don't plant new bulbs in the same site for at least three years in case of re-infection.

Narcissus fly attacks daffodils and narcissus bulbs, causing stunted growth and no flowers. The bulbs also become soft.

Tulip fire causes 'scorched' patches on the leaves and spots on the flowers. Tulips planted in wet ground are more susceptible to attack.

Virus diseases cause mottled distorted leaves and stunted growth.

Flowered bulbs should be dead-headed, with the exception of small bulbs that can be left to self-seed. For feeding see page 58.

Never cut off, twist or tie the dying leaves, but leave them loose to die back naturally so that the bulbs can store up reserves for next year. If it's essential to clear the ground before the leaves have completely died back, lift the bulbs carefully with a fork and replant them close together in a trench out of the way. They can then be lifted and stored in summer for replanting in autumn.

Climbers

Clematis montana varieties are very vigorous and they often outgrow their sites. Pruning should be done immediately after flowering to restrict growth as necessary. Don't prune again later in the year or you'll be cutting off next year's flowers.

C. alpina and *C. macropetala* can also be pruned now if they're overgrown.

Tie in shoots of all climbers regularly. Even self-clinging and twining ones sometimes need a bit of encouragement to head in the right direction.

Herbaceous Perennials and Alpines

Alpines like *Aubrieta* and *Arabis* that have become straggly should be trimmed back after flowering. Weed alpine beds regularly and top up the layer of fine gravel if necessary.

Spring-flowering perennials like lungwort (*Pulmonaria*) and leopard's bane (*Doronicum*) that have finished flowering should be cut back to ground level so that

---

TIPS FOR SUCCESSFUL CONTAINERS

- Put larger pots in position before planting.
- If containers are moveable and there's space in the greenhouse or conservatory, plant them up early in the month and leave them indoors for several weeks to get off to a flying start before they're moved outside. A sack barrow with inflatable tyres is useful as this will enable you to move even the largest pots, fully planted, on your own.
- Make sure that all containers have drainage holes or water will build up inside and rot the roots. Raise the pots 2.5 cm (1 in) or so off the ground to assist drainage further – use either pieces of wood or special 'pot feet' for terracotta pots. If you surround the feet with the grease sold for grease-banding fruit trees, you'll have no trouble from vine weevils.
- Put a 2.5–5-cm (1–2-in) thick layer of material like broken clay pots or coarse gravel in the bottom of the pot, which again improves drainage as it stops roots and compost clogging up the holes in the container.
- *Always* use fresh potting compost. Don't be tempted to skimp and use unsuitable materials like garden soil, the contents of old growing bags, peat or crushed bark. Bear in mind that as container-grown plants have limited root space, they need to get their roots into something good in order to perform well for months on end.
- Harden off plants raised under cover before planting out (see page 65).
- Start planting in the middle of the container and work outwards. Put in as many plants as possible for a really top-class display. Even then, push in two or three seeds of nasturtiums to continue the show until late autumn.
- Firm the compost gently when planting, but take care not to over-firm soilless composts in particular.
- Water thoroughly after planting and then whenever necessary. See page 101, for details on feeding, watering and aftercare.

they'll form a neat mound of new foliage. Untrimmed leaves are often ravaged by mildew. Evergreen perennials like elephant's ears (*Bergenia*) are best tidied up next month (see page 103).

Polyanthus and double primroses should be lifted after flowering and divided into single plants. Line them out in rows in a lightly shaded nursery bed to grow on until autumn, when they can be planted out in the borders again.

Herbaceous perennials can often be raised from seed. Popular plants that are easy to grow include *Achillea*, columbine (*Aquilegia*), *Delphinium*, globe thistle (*Echinops*), *Erigeron*, oriental poppy (*Papaver orientale*) and *Verbascum*. Seeds of certain plants like masterwort (*Astrantia*), *Dicentra* and *Sedum* need a cold period before they'll germinate, so either sow them in autumn or mix the seed with a little damp sand in a polythene bag and put it in the refrigerator for a month before sowing. This fools the seeds into thinking they've been through the winter.

Take out a shallow drill in a well-prepared seedbed, either outside or in a coldframe. Water the drill before sowing. If your soil is light, mix a little coir compost into the drill, which will help retain moisture, then water thoroughly. Sow the seed thinly and cover it lightly with soil. Label each row using long-lasting labels. During dry spells, water the seedlings using a fine spray.

Perennials grown from seed last year can be planted out once they're well established in a minimum pot size of 7.5 cm (3 in).

LAWN

Sow or turf new lawns as soon as possible, before the weather becomes too warm and dry for the new grass to establish properly. Lawns sown last month should be ready for their first cut (see page 61).

During dry spells, water newly sown or turfed lawns using a fine sprinkler. Check whether you need a licence.

Mow new and established lawns regularly as growth increases. Put the grass cuttings on the compost heap and mix them well with other coarser material or they'll become a soggy airless mass. Don't put grass clippings directly on borders as a mulch, because they heat up and this could damage the plants.

SHRUBS

Evergreen hedges that are formally shaped should be lightly trimmed towards the end of the month, including box (*Buxus sempervirens*), holly (*Ilex*), privet (*Ligustrum*) and *Lonicera nitida*. Shape the hedge so that it's wider at the bottom, which looks good and gives it added stability. For larger hedges, which can be difficult to cut level just by eye, it's often useful to make a guideline by running a length of string between canes to mark the height you want.

Such hedges are favourite nest sites for birds, so do watch out for nests and leave them undisturbed until the fledglings have flown.

Box and other evergreen hedges can now be given a light haircut. Shears are best for small hedges but powered clippers are a lot easier for tall hedges.

Bog primulas like P. pulverulenta create glorious drifts of spring and early summer colour. They often self-seed so you should end up with a substantial group.

Pyracantha that's trained against walls or fences should be pruned after flowering. Cut back all outward-pointing shoots to within two or three buds of last year's growth and tie in other shoots.

Seedlings of shrubs and trees can be pricked out or potted up. Shrubs should be potted individually into 7.5-cm (3-in)

pots once they're large enough to handle. Tree seedlings need a minimum pot size of 13 cm (5 in).

Tender shrubs in containers that have been over-wintered in the greenhouse or conservatory can now be moved outside for the summer. These 'inside-outside' plants are excellent value as they provide

a ready-made display for instant impact, year after year. They divide into two main groups: evergreens that are hardy in most winters but which can be scorched by frost, and shrubs on the borderline of hardiness that won't tolerate much, if any, frost. Early summer is a good time to buy and plant these shrubs.

Good evergreens for tubs include New Zealand flax (*Phormium*) which forms tall clumps of spiky leaves striped with red, cream or green; *Yucca* varieties with variegated leaves like 'Golden Sword' or 'Bright Edge'; and bay trees (*Laurus nobilis*) which can be trained as standards or pyramids. Bay leaves are wonderful for flavouring lots of different dishes.

Tender flowering shrubs include the shrubby musk (*Mimulus aurantiacus*) that produces exquisite peachy-apricot flowers from early summer to autumn; *Lantana camara* which bears rounded clusters of flowers of many shades, which are fragrant and popular with butterflies; *Coronilla valentina* 'Variegata' which has masses of fragrant golden flowers; and *Solanum rantonnetii* which produces many deep-purple-blue ones.

WATER GARDEN

Bog gardens should be weeded and tidied before the plants grow too large. Watch out for young seedlings of plants like *Primula* and Kaffir lily (*Schizostylis*), which can be potted up or transplanted.

Duckweed and fairy moss (*Azolla*) are tiny floating plants that should never be deliberately introduced to a pond because they're almost impossible to eradicate. However, if they're already in your pond, let them grow during early spring as they help suppress green algae. Once the oxygenating plants and water lilies are growing strongly, remove duckweed and fairy moss regularly using a net or an old kitchen sieve.

Fish should be fed regularly now the weather is warmer and they're becoming more active. Feed them once a day but provide only as much food as they can eat in about a quarter of an hour.

PLANT OF THE MONTH

Bleeding heart *(Dicentra spectabilis)*
HEIGHT: 60 cm (2 ft)
SPREAD: 45 cm (1½ ft)
FLOWERING TIME: May–June
POSITION: Partial shade
SOIL: Any with plenty of organic matter **HARDY?**: Yes

The tall, gracefully arching stems of deep pink and white flowers make this plant one of the most beautiful of all herbaceous perennials. The flowers dangle, locket-like, beneath the long stems, and their unusual shape has given rise to a wealth of common names: 'Dutchman's breeches', 'lady's locket' and even 'lady-in-the-bath'. The divided fern-like foliage also looks very pretty in early spring when it forms a neat fresh clump.

The whole plant dies back later in the summer, so put it with late summer-flowering perennials like Japanese anemone (*Anemone japonica*), Michaelmas daisy (*Aster*) and *Clematis heracleifolia*. They'll spread to cover the resulting bare patch of ground.

Kitchen garden

FRUIT

Codling moth can be controlled with pheromone traps hung at about head height from the branches of apple trees. During late May and June the moths lay their eggs (which hatch into maggots) inside the apples. The moths can be controlled by spraying, but trapping is a safe organic method which gives about 80 per cent control. The trap consists of a small plastic 'tent', into which is put a piece of sticky paper that's impregnated with the pheromone given off by female moths. The males are attracted and caught, so they can't fertilize the females and consequently there aren't any eggs laid. One trap protects up to five trees.

Strawberry fruits need to be lifted off the ground once small clusters of berries have started to form. Tuck straw under the leaves or use special strawberry mats. This stops the fruits from rotting on damp ground and protects them from rain-splashed soil and slugs. Delay this job until the latter half of the month

since straw insulates the plants from the heat in the soil which could protect them from late frosts. Keep birds off ripening fruit by laying netting or horticultural fleece over the crop. Take a few cloches off protected plants during the day to let insects pollinate the flowers.

HERBS

Mint can be lifted and divided into smaller pieces for replanting. Because it can be very invasive, it's best to restrict the roots (see page 44).

Perennial herbs like bay, rue and rosemary raised from cuttings taken last summer (see page 120) can now be planted out. Make regular sowings of frequently used herbs like parsley to be sure of a continuous supply.

VEGETABLES

Brassicas (members of the cabbage family) that are growing in a seedbed should be planted out when two adult leaves have formed. Space Brussels sprouts 60–75 cm (2–2½ ft) apart, calabrese 30 x 15 cm (12 x 6 in) apart, cabbages 45 cm (1½ ft) and cauliflowers 60 cm (2 ft). Protect all plants against cabbage root fly (see page 69).

Broad beans should have their succulent young tops pinched out once around five trusses of flowers have formed, otherwise they can become infested with blackfly.
  Support unstable plants using a line or two of string run between canes at each end of the row.

Cardoons (*Cynara cardunculus*) can be sown now. These tall handsome plants, related to globe artichokes, form spectacular clumps of bold grey-green leaves. Cardoons are often grown for their ornamental value alone, but they can be blanched in summer to produce fleshy edible stems.

Birds love strawberries even before they're ripe, so protect the plants with netting.

In milder districts the seed can be sown directly outside. Sow three seeds per station 45 cm (1½ ft) apart with 75 cm (2½ ft) between rows, and thin to one seedling per station. Otherwise sow the seed individually in small pots under glass. Ready-grown plants are sometimes sold by garden centres.

Carrot root fly is a common pest. The larvae tunnel into the roots, and they also attack celery, parsnips and parsley. The most effective protection is to cover the whole crop with horticultural fleece. The first carrot flies appear towards the end of the month, so the covering needs to be in place by mid-May. There's also a second generation in August, so remember to protect the later crop too.

This pest is attracted by the scent of carrots, and therefore it's best not to thin the crop if possible. Sow the seed sparingly, and if you do need to thin the seedlings, don't leave the thinnings lying nearby. Planting rows of onions between carrots can be useful as the strong onion smell overlays that of the carrots. There are also several varieties now on the market which are reasonably resistant to carrot fly, like 'Fly Away' and 'Sytan'.

Chicory for forcing can be sown in shallow drills 15 cm (6 in) apart. Thin seedlings to the same distance apart. This type of chicory is lifted in winter and forced to produce 'chicons'. The variety must be one specifically designed for forcing, such as 'Flash' or 'Apollo'. Don't confuse this type with radicchio, a leafy type of chicory that's sown next month.

Florence fennel sown last month should be thinned to 23 cm (9 in) apart. Water it well during any dry spells, as fennel will run to seed if it's short of water.

Globe artichokes sown in modules during March should be planted out, spaced 45 cm (1½ ft) apart. In the second year remove alternate seedlings to leave 1m (3 ft) between plants.

After three years the crop is usually exhausted and it should be replaced. Save the rooted offsets or suckers and replant them 1m (3 ft) apart or raise new plants. Those raised from March sowings crop later than those left in from last year, so it's possible to grow a succession. Suckers can also be bought from specialist suppliers.

Hoe regularly round all vegetables to keep down weeds while they're still small. Weeds can grow incredibly fast at this time of year and they'll take valuable water and nutrients away from young crops. Use a short-handled onion hoe to weed closely around plants.

Leeks sown in a seedbed can be transplanted when they're about pencil thickness. Use a dibber to make holes 15 cm (6 in) deep and the same distance apart,

By the middle of the month, cover carrots with horticultural fleece or perforated polythene to stop the first carrot flies laying their eggs next to the plants.

▶ *The vegetable plot needs attention little and often to keep the plants spaced, weeded and growing strongly. The delicious harvest makes it all worthwhile.*

with 30 cm (1 ft) between rows. Drop one plant in each hole. Don't refill it, but just water well to settle the soil around the roots. This deep planting helps produce a long white stem.

Leeks sown under cover in modules can be planted out, spaced 30 cm (1 ft) apart. These clusters of seedlings don't need deep planting or thinning because the wider spacing lets the plants push outwards as they grow and they will blanch each other.

Marrows and courgettes grown under cover can be planted out towards the end of the month in milder areas, spaced 60 cm (2 ft) apart. Harden them off first, and cover plants with cloches if there's any danger of late frosts. In colder areas delay planting until next month and give the

young plants a liquid feed to keep them growing strongly.

Seed can also be sown at the same spacing. Sow two seeds per station and thin to one seedling.

Plants growing under cloches can be gradually hardened off towards the end of the month. Remove the cloche ends during the day for a week or so, then remove several cloches in the daytime for another week, but still replace them at night. They can be taken off completely in June.

Spinach often runs to seed if it's sown after May. Leaf beet (often called perpetual spinach) and Swiss chard are more tolerant of hotter drier conditions and they can still be sown regularly.

Swedes used to be grown more or less exclusively for animal fodder, which understandably has put some people off! But modern varieties are different again and make delicious winter vegetables. Sow thinly in shallow rows 30 cm (1½ ft) apart. Swedes are slow to mature, so they should be sown by the middle of June to give them enough time to grow.

Sweetcorn plants raised inside can be planted out in a sheltered sunny site towards the end of the month after they've been hardened off. Because the plants need to pollinate each other, it's best to put them in blocks rather than in rows, spaced 45 cm (1½ ft) apart.

Where space is limited, sow a quick growing crop like lettuce or radish between the plants. Marrows and courgettes or a soil-improving green-manure crop like mustard can also be grown between the sweetcorn plants.

Vegetables to sow in rows include beetroot, carrots, French beans, parsnips, runner beans, salad vegetables, salsify and scorzonera. Thin out vegetables sown earlier in rows.

In a seedbed early in the month, sow autumn cauliflower, calabrese, kale and kohl rabi.

COMPOSTING

This month most gardens will produce piles of grass cuttings and buckets of weeds. Never throw them away. They can be recycled back to the soil, adding precious plant food and creating a home for billions of friendly soil organisms. This kind of bulky organic matter is the very basis of fertility and the difference between a hard, unyielding, difficult soil and a crumbly, easily worked and super-productive one.

First you need two compost containers, one to fill up while the stuff in the other one is rotting down. You can buy them at any garden centre or make them yourself. A good container consists of a box about 75 cm (2½ ft) square by 1 m (3 ft) high with a lid and a removable front for access. Buy or make one that has no air holes in the sides and a lid to keep rain out and heat in.

Anything at all can go on the heap, though avoid cooked food, the roots of perennial weeds like docks and bindweed, and woody material.

Best of all is grass, but it's essential to mix it with coarser stuff to ensure that there's plenty of air in it. So put in a 23 cm (9 in) layer, cover it with 15 cm (6 in) of coarser material and mix it up a bit with a fork. If you haven't enough coarse material, buy a bag of fresh horse manure.

After a month turn the compost by throwing it out of the bin and then back in, fluffing it up as you go. Then put the lid back on and leave it for another two months to produce rich, brown, crumbly, sweet-smelling *fertility*. And all for nothing.

Greenhouse and windowsill

Greenhouse vegetables like tomatoes, cucumbers, peppers and aubergines can be planted out into growing bags, large pots, or directly into the greenhouse soil. Established plants that were set out earlier should be fed twice weekly with liquid tomato fertilizer.

Train tomatoes up strings (see below) and stake all other plants using bamboo canes and plant ties.

Once tomato flowers open, give their pollination a helping hand by shaking the plants gently or spraying the flowers with water from a hand sprayer.

Half-hardy annuals to grow as autumn- and winter-flowering pot plants can be sown now. *Browallia, Calceolaria, Cineraria, Clarkia* and poor man's orchid (*Schizanthus*) should be sown thinly in pots or trays at a temperature of 18°C (65°F). Prick out the seedlings into 7.5-cm (3-in) pots when they're large enough to handle.

Half-hardy annuals for planting outside can still be sown regularly with the exception of plants like begonias and busy Lizzies (*Impatiens*) which need a long growing season. Making several sowings from early to late spring will ensure a succession of colour right through the autumn, either in the borders or in pots for the house.

Hanging baskets and containers of frost-tender plants can be planted up in a greenhouse or conservatory and grown on under cover until next month, when they can be moved outdoors. This'll give your containers a flying start, especially

GROWING AND TRAINING TOMATOES

1 *Young tomato plants can be grown on in pots in the greenhouse until they're well established. Don't overcrowd them, or they'll reach for the light and become thin and leggy.*

2 *When planting them out into growing bags, large pots or the greenhouse soil, support them by running a length of nylon string underneath the rootball and fastening the other end to the greenhouse structure directly above.*

in colder areas where they shouldn't go outside until the middle of the month.

Pests and diseases can start to take a hold as the weather becomes warmer, so inspect all greenhouse plants regularly. Look underneath the leaves for whitefly and check the soft young shoots for greenfly. Picking off and squashing isolated groups of pests by hand can often nip a severe attack 'in the bud' without resorting to other means of control. Hang several yellow sticky traps around the greenhouse to catch any pests, though not if predatory insects have been introduced. See page 48 for pest control.

Tender perennials can still be propagated by cuttings (see page 73). Pot on rooted cuttings and young plants once they've rooted round their existing pots, until they're large enough to plant out. Pinch out their tips to encourage lots of bushy growth.

Vegetables can still be sown indoors to shorten the overall growing time, including courgettes, cucumbers, marrows, melons, pumpkins, runner beans, squashes and sweetcorn. They can also be sown directly outside. Do both at the beginning of the month.

Ornamental cabbages and kales are striking and unusual plants for winter bedding displays. Their frilled leaves are red or green, and white, and more brightly coloured in the centre. The colours intensify when night temperatures start to fall in autumn. The F1 hybrids such as 'Red Peacock', 'White Peacock', 'Cherry Sundae' and 'Xmas Bouquet' are best as they develop more evenly and uniformly.

Sow the seeds individually in 7.5-cm (3-in) pots of coir compost at a temperature of 18°C (65°F). Grow them on in good light and pot them up into 13-cm (5-in) pots once they're well established.

3 *Gently wind the plants around the string as they grow. As sideshoots appear in the leaf joints, snap them off while they're young. Break off the bottom leaves when they've turned yellow.*

CHECKLIST

- Tie in briar fruits regularly.
- Plant evergreens by the end of the month.
- Sow salad vegetables every two to three weeks for a constant supply.
- Weed and mulch borders if you did not do so earlier.
- Prune shrubs like *Kerria* that have flowered (see page 105).
- Continue taking basal cuttings of herbaceous perennials.
- Remove blanketweed regularly from ponds.
- Plant and divide aquatics as described on page 65.
- Finish planting tubers like dahlias and begonias.
- Protect young plants against slugs.
- Paint the greenhouse with shading if you did not do this earlier.
- Stake and tie perennials regularly as they grow.
- Start hardening off plants raised under cover

JUNE

THERE'S SIMPLY NO BETTER place to be in June than in your own garden. A great mass of young foliage and flower will fill your days with colour and perfume and you'll come in at twilight with a heart full of joy and satisfaction.

The vegetable garden should now be providing enough to make trips to the greengrocer unnecessary and there should be plenty of soft fruit too. If you think that gardeners' eulogies of freshly dug potatoes and sun-warmed strawberries are over-stated, try growing a few of your own. If you harvest them just a few minutes before they're needed, there's simply no comparison with the stale old supermarket stuff. With a little effort you really can live like a king.

◀ *The garden is chock-full of flowers in July. The old-fashioned Portland rose 'Comte de Chambord' looks gorgeous against the tall blue spires of delphiniums.*

GARDENS TO VISIT

- **Abbotsbury Gardens**, Dorset. A paradise of sub-tropical plants. Many huge trees, including unusual and tender specimens. Lots of other unusual plants. Plant centre.
- **The Gardens of the Rose**, St Albans, Hertfordshire. Gardens of the Royal National Rose Society. An excellent place to visit with notebook and camera, especially if looking for new roses. Approximately 1700 different varieties!
- **Inverewe**, Wester Ross, Scotland. The warm Gulf Stream plus strategic planting of shelter trees enable many tender plants to be grown, from countries including South America, Australia and China. Palms, tree ferns, eucalyptus, huge rhododendrons. Shop, restaurant and plants for sale.
- **Wallington Gardens**, Northumberland. Historic walled garden packed with informal plantings. Many hectares of parkland including woods and lakes. Large conservatory of exotic tender plants. House (open), shop and café.

Looking good

Shrubs in flower are numerous this month. The earliest *Buddleia* species usually attract some butterflies, though there'll be far more later in summer when the butterfly bush (*Buddleia davidii*) flowers. One of the best is *B. alternifolia* with pale lilac flowers in small clusters along its graceful arching branches. *B. globosa* and *B.* x *weyeriana* 'Sungold' are more showy with bright orange-yellow 'balls' of flowers. For mild areas and sheltered sites, *B. caryopteridifolia* has lilac-pink clusters of fragrant flowers and attractive 'woolly' white leaves. These tall deciduous shrubs look good at the back of the border or planted on their own.

One shrub that definitely needs to be planted as a single specimen is the magnificent wedding cake bush (*Viburnum plicatum*). This large shrub forms tiers of branches, the top side of which are covered with creamy-white flowers in May and June. The varieties 'Lanarth', 'Mariesii' and 'Summer Snowflake' are all excellent, and 'Watanabe' is compact and suitable for small gardens. Also flowering now is *V. sargentii* 'Onondaga' which has purplish green lobed leaves that contrast well with its white flowers.

For the smaller garden, *Abelia* varieties deserve to be grown more widely. These compact evergreen shrubs produce masses of flowers through summer and often well into autumn. *A. schumannii* and 'Edward Goucher' have lilac-pink flowers, *A.* x *grandiflora* bears pale pink ones, as does 'Francis Mason' which also has gold-flushed leaves. Abelias like sun and prefer a sheltered site.

There are many other shrubs flowering now, like sun rose (*Cistus*), *Cotoneaster*, *Escallonia*, *Genista*, *Hebe*, *Phlomis*, *Potentilla*, *Santolina*, *Senecio*, *Spiraea*, *Tamarix* and *Weigela*.

Fragrant shrubs can be enjoyed to the full in summer. Scent adds an extra dimension to the garden, and to get the full benefit put fragrant plants near a patio or seat, alongside a frequently used pathway or close to your windows and doors. Grow a few smaller plants in tubs so that they can be easily moved to the best positions.

Roses are top of the list for fragrance this month, and there's an enormous range to choose from. To find the ones you like best it's a good idea to browse through some catalogues, then visit a few gardens and nurseries and make a note of your preferred varieties. Climbing and rambler roses look wonderful round doors and windows, or scrambling over arches and pergolas, and of course the blooms are just at the right level to smell. Ramblers are vigorous plants ideal for covering a big space fast, but most flower only once. Climbers are less vigorous but flower repeatedly throughout the summer. Good scented ramblers include 'Albertine' (coppery-pink) and 'Seagull' (white). 'Wedding Day' (creamy-yellow fading to white) is lovely but extremely vigorous. Good climbers include 'Crimson Glory' (deep crimson), 'Gloire de Dijon' (buff-yellow), 'Mme Alfred Carrière' (white flushed with pink) and 'Maigold' (bronze-yellow).

Many old-fashioned shrub roses are beautifully scented. To find a wide selection of true old roses you'll probably have to go to a specialist nursery and order your plants for autumn delivery. Many of the oldest roses like the Gallica, Damask, Alba and Centifolia roses have only one burst of flowers, which is fine if there's space for lots of plants. Otherwise choose ones which will repeat-flower, like the Bourbon, China, Portland and Hybrid perpetual roses. There are also modern shrub roses like Rugosas and Hybrid musks. 'English' roses are a new breed which combine the best of the new and old, with scented flowers shaped like the old-fashioned varieties but repeat-flowering.

Lavender is wonderfully fragrant, and it makes a fine dwarf hedge to line a pathway or edge a rose border. Mock orange (*Philadelphus*) is an easy-to-grow shrub with just about the sweetest scent of all. 'Virginal' is widely sold but this variety is only for the larger garden. For small spaces consider some of the more compact ones like 'Manteau d'Hermine', 'Avalanche', 'Frosty Morn' or *P. micro-phyllus*.

Climbers and wall shrubs also include many fragrant varieties. Honeysuckles (*Lonicera*) bear many colourful clusters of flowers. These adaptable plants are happy in most situations, but they do best with their roots in the shade and their heads in the sun. The most tolerant species is Japanese honeysuckle (*L. japonica* 'Halliana'). It keeps its leaves in all but the worst winters, and its rampant growth is ideal for screening. Don't be afraid to chop this variety hard back if it gets too large. Other good honeysuckle varieties include *L.* x *americana* and *L. periclymenum* 'Belgica' and 'Graham Thomas'. The leaves of *L. P.* 'Harlequin' are attractively variegated with cream, pink and green.

Californian lilacs (*Ceanothus*) produce stunning blue flowers which are so intensely coloured that they look almost unreal. These sun-loving shrubs are happiest when they're trained against a south-facing sheltered wall or fence, on well-drained soil. The best varieties are *C. impressus*, 'Puget Blue', *C. thyrsiflorus* and *C. veitchianus*.

Gold flowers contrast well with blue. If the wall's large enough, plant a Californian lilac with one of its compatriots, *Fremontodendron* 'California Glory'. It bears large, waxy, bright golden flowers in bursts throughout summer. The evergreen laburnum (*Piptanthus nepalensis*) does well against a wall too. It has dangling clusters of yellow flowers that are shown off perfectly against its dark green, lobed, evergreen leaves.

Herbaceous perennials are looking really good now, with many plants in flower and others forming neat clumps of fresh foliage. There are lots of the popular, old, 'cottage-garden' plants like columbine or granny's bonnets (*Aquilegia*) with their multi-coloured spurred flower heads. 'Woodside' is a new variety which has leaves speckled

THE GARDEN INDOORS

MAKE YOUR OWN POT-POURRI

Bowls of fragrant pot-pourri are easy to make, and they're a wonderful way of bringing the garden's perfume into the house all year round. Their delicate lingering fragrance is far more pleasant than the smell of those ghastly chemical air fresheners.

Any scented flowers or leaves can be used to make pot-pourri. Fragrant flowers include roses, lavender, violets, broom, pinks, jasmine, honeysuckle and wallflowers. Plants with aromatic foliage include lemon verbena, lemon balm, eau-de-cologne mint and pelargoniums with scented leaves. For extra colour add a few flowers of marigolds, pot marigolds, love-in-a-mist,

cornflowers or sweet peas.

Pick the flowers and leaves early in the day when the weather's dry. Choose flowers that are nearly, but not quite fully open. Spread the flowers and foliage to dry outside on wire mesh that's fixed above the ground to let the air circulate thoroughly, or put them on trays in a very low oven with the door open.

When the material is dry and crisp to the touch, mix it together in a large bowl with some chopped citrus peel and about half a cup of powdered orris root to 'fix' the fragrance. Store it in an airtight container for a month or so, then put it in decorative bowls or jars around the house.

PLANT OF THE MONTH

Ornamental onion *(Allium christophii)*
HEIGHT: 60 cm (2 ft)
SPREAD: 30 cm (1 ft)
FLOWERING TIME: May–June
POSITION: Sun
SOIL: Well-drained **HARDY?**: Yes

A name like 'ornamental onion' doesn't really do justice to the many superb varieties of the Allium family. One of the most handsome is A. christophii. It bears huge rounded heads of flowers around 25 cm (10 in) across, made up of hundreds of spiky, steely violet-purple petals. They can be dried easily and used in flower arrangements. To conceal their dying foliage, put them behind perennials or small shrubs like purple sage (*Salvia purpurascens*) or *Artemisia* 'Powis Castle'. The flowers look lovely with purple foliage, like the *Cotinus* in the picture.

Allium bulbs are sold in autumn and should be planted 10 cm (4 in) deep. There are many other handsome varieties of various heights with white, yellow, pink, purple and even blue flowers, all of which are well worth growing.

with white. It's one of those 'love it or hate it' plants. Perennial forget-me-not (*Brunnera macrophylla*) bears stems of blue flowers and rounded leaves that make good ground cover and it thrives in the shade. Herbaceous geraniums are excellent easy plants that are also good for ground cover, and many of those will do well in shade too. Lady's mantle (*Alchemilla mollis*) has beautiful scalloped leaves and froths of lime-green flowers, but cut the dead flowers off if you don't want it to seed itself everywhere – not a bad problem to have though! All these plants are low-growing, front of the border plants, though there are others which are especially good for edging. *Heuchera* varieties form neat, rounded clumps of scalloped leaves of several colours. 'Rachel' and 'Palace Purple' have attractive purple leaves, while those of 'Pewter Moon' are marbled with silver. They look especially good with dark pink *Dianthus* and silver-foliaged plants like *Artemisia* and *Anthemis tinctoria*. Catmint (*Nepeta*) is a lovely edging plant where its masses of blue-mauve flowers can spill over onto a path, as can be seen in the picture on page 95.

Flag irises (*Iris germanica*) are useful as their spiky leaves create a good contrast to many other perennials, and the tall stems of honey-scented flowers make a glorious display. There's a whole range of colours available, so choose your plants in flower or go to a specialist nursery for the best selection. For a really stunning contrasting shape in a large sunny border, *Crambe cordifolia* produces 1.8-m- (6-ft)-tall stems that form giant clouds of small white flowers.

Other perennials flowering now include *Achillea, Astilbe, Astrantia, Geum*, peonies and *Verbascum*.

▶ *The luscious globe flowers of peonies and those of the small* Dianthus *go well with purple-leaved sage. Peonies are best planted in the middle of the border so that other plants conceal their dying foliage later in summer.*

General tasks

Cut flowers from the garden are often infested with small black pollen beetles, which tend to invade garden plants once oilseed rape has been harvested. The beetles are harmless, but they're a nuisance inside the house in large numbers. Clear them off cut flowers by leaving the bunches in a dark garage or shed for a couple of hours – the beetles will fly to the window in search of light.

Late frosts can check and even kill newly planted half-hardy annuals and tender vegetable plants. If frost is forecast, protect plants overnight using polythene, fleece or fine windbreak netting. Newspaper can be made into 'hats' for individual plants like runner beans, though they are a bit of a fiddle to hold down with soil or pebbles.

Mulches can be applied at any time of year. They're excellent for reducing water loss from the soil in summer, but do make sure that the ground is damp before putting on a mulch or rain will take a long time to get through. See page 35 for different types of mulch.

Water thoroughly during dry spells, concentrating on new plants, those in containers, and climbers against walls and fences where the soil tends to be dry. Pay special attention to dahlias, sweet peas, gladioli and fruit bushes.

Weeds should be hoed off while they're still young. Hoeing is best done on hot days when the weeds will die quickly. Dig up perennial weeds before they have a chance to establish.

▲ *Take care when hoeing around young plants – it's easy to chop them off! Hand-weeding close to the rows is often best.*

▶ *Chipped bark is an excellent and widely available mulch, and it really sets off the plants well too.*

Ornamental garden

ANNUALS, BIENNIALS AND TENDER PERENNIALS

Hardy annuals can still be sown to give colour from mid-summer to autumn. Choose fast-growing varieties like stocks, *Clarkia*, *Godetia*, candytuft (*Iberis*), pot marigold (*Calendula*) and toadflax (*Linaria*).

Containers and hanging baskets can now be planted up, or moved outside if they were planted last month. All containers need regular care and attention:
• Water them regularly. Remember that there's a lot of plants growing in a confined space and they're entirely reliant on you for water. Rain is *never* enough.

Containers usually need watering every day in warm weather and sometimes even twice a day later in the summer. There's more air movement around hanging baskets, so they dry out faster than tubs.

If you're often away from home, or if you have a lot of containers, consider installing an automatic watering system. There are several good systems available which will save a lot of time and perhaps a bit of heartbreak too.
• Water first thing in the morning or in the evening if possible, rather than in hot sun. Water splashes can result in scorched flowers and foliage.

SUCCESSFUL HANGING PLANTS

There are lots of different hanging baskets to choose from. The best type is an open mesh basket which can be planted on the sides as well as the top. Cram in as many plants as possible for a really top-class display. As well as traditional hanging baskets, there are terracotta wall pots in lots of designs and 'manger' style wall troughs. 'Swags' are a wonderful way of growing plants against a wall. They're tough bags which are filled with compost, then you cut slits in the bag through which to put the plants. After growing them on for a couple of weeks, they can be hung in their final position.

Always use a good potting compost. It's well worth adding a controlled-release fertilizer before planting. Although it's a little expensive, it gives good results and there's no need for additional liquid feeding until late summer.

There's a vast range of summer-flowering plants available in many colours, so you can make up your favourite colour schemes.

Geraniums are available both as trailing ivy-leaved varieties, and upright types suitable for planting in the centre of the basket. The main colours are red, pink and white, though there are lots of different shades.

Fuchsias are also available in trailing and bush forms, with both single and double flowers in an enormous range of colours. Fuchsias dislike too much sun, as do busy Lizzies (*Impatiens*), so they're ideal for a cooler shady site.

Petunias come in a wide range of colours. The new 'Surfina' trailing petunias are superb hanging basket plants that provide masses of colour.

Tuberous begonias are excellent in baskets. The tubers can be bought and potted individually earlier in spring to get them off to a flying start (see page 21). Pendulous begonias provide a cascade of colour, while upright varieties make good plants for the centre of the basket. But these slightly fragile plants are only for a sheltered spot.

Tender perennials include some marvellous trailing plants that make a long-lasting and unusual display of flowers, like *Bidens ferulaefolia*, swan river daisy (Brachycome), *Lysimachia congestiflora*, *Portulaca*, *Scaevola* and *Verbena* x *hybrida*. *Lotus berthelotii* has claw-shaped, dark red flowers and its needle-like silver leaves are particularly attractive. Plants with cool foliage colours provide an excellent foil: *Helichrysum petiolare* has silver, lime-green and variegated leaves, *Nepeta* produces long trails of leaves, and *Lysimachia nummularia* 'Aurea' has yellow leaves and golden flowers. The latter two are usually hardy.

PLANTING UP A HANGING BASKET

Hanging baskets can be planted and put outside this month. If there's room in the greenhouse, they can be planted up in May and grown under cover for several weeks.

1 *Line a mesh basket with a coir, wool or plastic liner, and put a circle of plastic in the bottom to help keep the moisture in.*

2 *Sit the basket on a large pot to keep it stable. Fill it with compost and, starting in the centre, fill round with lower growing plants, including trailing plants at the edges.*

3 *Hang the basket on a stout bracket which is securely fixed to the wall. Push trailing plants through the coir, so the whole basket will be a globe of colour. Water it thoroughly.*

• Feed twice weekly once plants have become established and they're growing strongly. Use a high-potash liquid feed like tomato fertilizer. If a slow-release fertilizer was mixed into the compost, liquid feeding will usually be necessary only as a top-up towards the end of the summer.

• Dead-head plants at least once a week to encourage plenty of flowers.

BULBS AND TUBERS

Lily beetle is becoming a problem, particularly in southern areas. Both adult beetles and their larvae attack lilies. They're very easy to identify because the adult beetles are bright red, and the orange-brown grubs surround themselves with black slime. The grubs are usually found under the leaves or in the joints. Inspect plants regularly and pick off and destroy the insects by hand, or spray with an insecticide containing permethrin.

CLIMBERS

Layering is a good way of propagating many climbers. Some plants like winter and summer jasmine and honeysuckle will layer themselves naturally, so have a look round the base of the plant for ready-rooted shoots that can be pegged down into pots. Once they've grown a good root system – in about a couple of months – they can be detached and planted elsewhere.

Serpentine layering is a method of producing several plants from one long shoot. Dig a little compost and sand into the soil and lay the shoot along the ground. Wound the stem just before each leaf joint (as for simple layering; see page 42) and peg it to the ground. Cover each pegged point with a little soil.

Plants that can be propagated in this way include clematis, honeysuckle (*Lonicera*), Virginia creeper (*Parthenocissus*) and ornamental vines (*Vitis*). *Wisteria* can also be layered, but the resulting plants could take a few years to flower and it's probably better to buy grafted plants.

HERBACEOUS PERENNIALS AND ALPINES

Alpines that are bare in the centre can be encouraged to regrow. Mix some coir compost with an equal amount of coarse grit and good garden soil and work it well into the bare centre. The plant will grow back into the fresh compost.

Older plants that are very bare in the centre can be rejuvenated by division, just like herbaceous plants. Simply dig up the plant, gently break it into several pieces and replant the younger pieces from the outside of the clump.

Evergreen perennials should be tidied up. Flowered stems of *Euphorbia robbiae* and *E. wulfenii* should be removed completely at ground level when they start to look tatty: this will help to keep the clump growing strongly. Wear gloves when you're handling euphorbias as the milky sap can cause skin rashes. Remove old and tattered leaves of evergreens like elephant's ears (*Bergenia*) and the Lenten rose (*Helleborus*).

Flag irises (*Iris germanica*) which are several years old are best divided once they've formed a clump of thick fleshy rhizomes on the surface of the soil. After flowering lift the clump carefully and remove younger pieces of rhizome with a sharp knife, making sure that each piece has plenty of roots. Discard the oldest pieces. Replant the divisions in groups of three or five in a sunny position, first trimming the leaves in half to prevent wind-rocking. The top part of the rhizome should be just above ground

Honeysuckle bears a profusion of beautifully-scented flowers, and it can easily be propagated by layering. This variety is the early Dutch honeysuckle, Lonicera periclymenum *'Belgica'.*

103

level. If you replant on the same spot, it is important to revitalize the soil first with a bucketful of garden compost and a handful of organic fertilizer.

Hellebores can be propagated from seed, which should be collected and sown while it's still green. If left to ripen, it can take months or even years to ger-minate. Sow thinly in trays, cover lightly with a little compost and stand the trays in a coldframe or a shaded sheltered place. The sap around the seed has been known to irritate the skin, so wash your hands afterwards.

LAWN

Established lawns should be fed with a liquid fertilizer if the grass is beginning to look tired and a little yellow. During long periods of dry weather, raise the height of the mower blades a little as the longer grass will be more able to tolerate drought.

Remove clumps of coarse grass using an old knife (see page 62).

Long grass where you've naturalized bulbs should be mown once the bulb foliage has turned brown and died back. Wild-flower lawns and meadows should also be mown for the first time at the beginning of the month, once the spring-flowering plants have set seed.

Perennial weeds in established lawns can be kept within bounds by raking the grass with a springtine rake just before mowing. This brings up the runners of weeds like buttercup which are then cut off by the mower. It won't kill them, but at least it stops them taking over.

ROSES

Dead-head all roses after flowering to encourage them to produce more flow-ers. When all the flowers on a single stem have died, cut it back by half to just above a bud to encourage another shoot and more flowers later in summer.

Pests and diseases often start to appear in earnest this month. Pick off and destroy any rolled-up leaves which will probably contain sawfly larvae. Lady-birds and other natural predators can usually deal with other pests.

If you're not averse to chemicals, spray severe attacks of greenfly. Continue spraying fortnightly with copper fungi-cide as a preventative measure against blackspot (see page 62). A combined

---

THE PRODUCTIVE GARDEN

Many gardens these days simply don't have room for a separate fruit and vegetable plot, but that shouldn't stop you growing them.

My strong advice would be to get yourself an allotment. Where else could you find your own 'place in the country' where you can relax at weekends, grow enough veg. and fruit for yourself and your family and reap the benefits of help, advice and friendship from a smashing lot of people? And all for about two bob a week!

But, failing that, there's no reason why you shouldn't grow fruit against your fences and walls, and vegetables in among the flowers in the borders.

Fruit trees ready-trained as fans, espaliers and cordons are available and are quite easy to grow against the fence where they take up very little space.

Vegetables can be grown in 'bays' left at the front of the border. Just fork over a small patch, working in a little garden compost and a handful of organic fertilizer. Scratch shallow drills 15–30 cm (6–12 in) apart with a stick and sow them thinly with lettuce or radish, onions, carrots, spinach, cabbage or cauliflowers. Thin them out to the same distances when they're big enough and you'll harvest rich rewards. They look great among the flowers and they'll rarely be attacked by pests or diseases.

Pruning spring-flowering deciduous shrubs

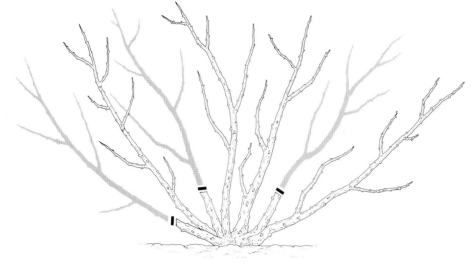

insecticide/fungicide spray can be used to control both pests and diseases.

Ramblers should have their new strong shoots tied in regularly before they become woody and inflexible.

Suckers should be removed as soon as they appear from the ground near the base of a rose. They come from the rootstock, which is a different inferior type of rose, and they're quite easy to recognize by their different leaves. Try to trace each one back to where it grows from the main stem and hoick it out by tugging downwards. If you can't get at this growing point, you'll have to cut the suckers, but that could mean that they'll regrow.

SHRUBS

Deciduous shrubs that have just flowered can now be pruned if they're becoming overgrown, including *Deutzia*, beauty bush (*Kolkwitzia*), mock orange (*Philadelphus*), *Kerria* and *Weigela*. Take out approximately a quarter to a third of the oldest branches as near as possible to ground level, and remove any dead, diseased or damaged stems at the same time. A curved pruning saw is ideal for this job.

Broom (*Cytisus*) can also be pruned in the same way. However, it's a fast-growing and relatively short-lived shrub, so it's usually best to replace old leggy plants with new ones.

Eucalyptus grown from seed in spring should be planted out when they're about 20–30 cm (8–12 in) high. Planting when they're small enables them to develop a good strong root system, so they won't need staking.

Layers of shrubs that were prepared last summer should be carefully inspected. Provided that a good root system has formed, cut the layer from its parent shrub and plant it elsewhere in the garden or pot it up. If there's not much root growth, leave it undisturbed for a couple more months.

Shrubs that can be layered include *Camellia*, dogwood (*Cornus*), *Daphne*, *Forsythia*, *Magnolia*, *Rhododendron*, lilac (*Syringa*) and *Viburnum*.

Overgrown evergreens can also be thinned out now. Prune out two or three of the oldest branches, but take care that you don't spoil the shape of the bush.

Rhododendrons that have flowered should be dead-headed regularly to encourage new growth. Snap the dead flowers off by hand, taking care not to damage the new shoots that are underneath the flower head.

Deep blue iris with Mimulus 'Wisley Red' make a handsome combination. The glossy water lily leaves complete the picture, but their dense growth will shortly be in need of thinning.

WATER GARDEN

Tender floating aquatics like water hyacinth (*Eichhornia crassipes*) that have been over-wintered inside can now be put back in the pond. This is also the best time to buy new floating plants.

Fish are best introduced to the pond in spring and summer. They're usually transported in polythene bags and they should be brought home as quickly as possible because the oxygen in the bag is limited. Float the bag in the pond for a short while before tipping the fish in so that the temperatures equalize.

Pond weeds like duckweed and blanketweed should be removed regularly. Pull out blanketweed by hand, or wind it around a bamboo cane. Leave it by the water's edge for a couple of days before composting it.

Kitchen garden

FRUIT

Black currants can suffer from a virus called 'reversion', which distorts leaves and makes them smaller than usual. Severely affected bushes should be dug up and burnt. Replace them with certified virus-free stock from a fruit specialist. The virus is transmitted by black currant gall mite (see page 66), so controlling the mite stops the plants becoming infected in the first place.

Fruit trees naturally shed their surplus amounts of fruit this month or early in July, hence the name 'June drop'. Unless the crop is sparse, it helps to thin the fruit further so that the remaining ones grow larger and are of better quality. Remove any damaged or misshapen fruits too.

Gooseberries carrying a heavy crop can also be thinned for the same reason.

Sawfly caterpillars can quickly destroy the foliage. Inspect the bushes regularly and spray with derris at the first sign of the black-spotted green caterpillars.

Strawberries produce many new shoots or runners which can be pegged down into 7.5-cm (3-in) pots of compost. They'll root quickly to make new plants that can be cut off and planted out in autumn. To stop the plants wasting their energy, cut off all runners that aren't wanted for propagation.

Long spells of wet weather encourage the growth of grey mould (*Botrytis*) on the fruit, which can quickly spread to ruin much of the crop. Inspect the fruits regularly and remove any infected ones. Put them in the dustbin, not on the compost heap.

HERBS

Containers of herbs make a lovely patio display as well as being handy for the kitchen, but not all herbs are suitable for containers. Some, like angelica and lovage, grow very tall.

Herbs with colourful foliage look good all summer. The sages *Salvia* 'Tricolor' with cream, green and purple leaves and *S.* 'Icterina' with golden ones are just as good in the kitchen as the plain green variety. The unusually shaped purple flowers of French lavender (*Lavandula stoechas*) make a good contrast, as does curry plant (*Helichrysum serotinum*) with its bright silvery foliage. Look out, too, for golden lemon balm, thymes with coloured foliage, marjoram, and garlic chives which has starch-white flowers. Mint is excellent in containers, but give it a pot to itself or it'll smother everything else. Parsley is also best on its own as it likes a cool partly-shaded position, while most herbs are sun-lovers.

VEGETABLES

Asparagus should be given an organic fertilizer after harvesting. Let the foliage grow so that the crowns can build up strength for next year's crop.

*Golden lemon balm (*Melissa officinalis *'Aurea') has attractive foliage and looks lovely in a pot. A simple combination of the balm together with clumps of green-leaved thyme and purple sage look extremely effective.*

Watch out for asparagus beetle, which has an orange body and chequered black and yellow wings. It can quickly destroy the growing ferns. Control it by spraying with derris.

Brassicas are often attacked by the caterpillars of the cabbage white butterfly. Nip the attack in the bud by inspecting the undersides of the leaves and squashing any clusters of black eggs or young caterpillars. Alternatively spray with the parasitic bacterium *Bacillus thuringiensis*. Regular severe attacks can be prevented by covering the whole crop with fleece, which stops the butterflies laying their eggs.

Celery can be planted out. Blanching varieties need to be planted in trenches prepared earlier (see page 69) and spaced 30 cm (1 ft) apart. Self-blanching celery doesn't need trenching, but plant it in a block with 23 cm (9 in) between plants so that they blanch each other.

Peas that have been harvested should be cut down to ground level. Leave the roots in as they will add useful nitrogen to the soil.

Potatoes planted in March should be ready to harvest. Lift one plant carefully with a fork to check if they're ready and then harvest as required. For the very best flavour, lift them just before they're needed. Most potatoes grow around the stem of the plant, but sift through the soil to check that they've all been lifted. Any overlooked tubers will be a nuisance when they grow next year.

Radicchio (chicory) can be sown in rows 23 cm (9 in) apart to harvest for autumn and winter salads. Choose a variety with coloured foliage for the best effect, like 'Palla Rossa' with red leaves or 'Alouette' that has red and white leaves.

Chicory sown last month for forcing should be thinned to 15 cm (6 in) apart.

Runner beans raised under cover can be planted out, preferably in prepared trenches (see page 22). Put up the supporting canes before planting, either in double rows or wigwams with 30 cm (1 ft) between each cane and 60 cm (2 ft) between rows. Seed can also be sown outside. Put collars made from plastic bottles around new plants to protect them from slugs.

Runner beans also look very good on wigwams in ornamental borders or growing up pergolas and arches. A variety like 'Painted Lady' with very decorative red-and-white flowers looks terrific.

Salad vegetables should be sown in small quantities every two to three weeks for a constant supply.

Try some of the less common varieties like celtuce, with leaves that can be eaten like lettuce and a stem that's delicious raw or cooked like celery. Salad rocket has a pleasantly spicy taste. Endive has attractively curled lettuce-like leaves, but it needs to be blanched in summer otherwise it's tough and bitter. Chinese radish produces large, round, colourful roots about the size and colour of a cricket ball. Sow the seed thinly in rows 23 cm (9 in) apart.

It is important to remember that lettuce won't germinate at high temperatures, so in hot weather sow the seed in the shade or in seedtrays and put them in a cool shady place.

Tomatoes can now be planted outside, spaced 45 cm (1½ ft) apart, in growing bags or in well-prepared ground. They like a sunny sheltered site and they'll do best against a south-facing wall. Stake the plants with 1.2-m (4-ft) bamboo canes and tie them loosely with soft string. Water them in well. Never let tomatoes go short of water as fluctuations in supply can cause the fruits to split.

Turnips can be sown in rows 15 cm (6 in) apart for an autumn crop. They dislike overcrowding, so thin them as soon as the first adult leaves appear to leave 10 cm (4 in) between plants. They'll need to be pulled quite young, but that's certainly when they're at their best.

Greenhouse and windowsill

Pinks (*Dianthus*) can be propagated by cuttings called 'pipings'. Select healthy young shoots and, holding the stem about three or four leaves down, just pull off the top part. It'll come away cleanly at the leaf joint you're holding. Put several cuttings round the edge of a 13-cm (5-in) pot of moist coir compost mixed 50/50 with vermiculite, and place the pots in a shaded coldframe. The cuttings should start to root fairly quickly and can then be potted individually into 7.5-cm (3-in) pots.

Houseplants can be moved into the greenhouse for a summer holiday and the hardier ones will benefit from going outside. Plants like azaleas, hydrangeas and citrus will certainly gain from this treatment, but make sure that you put them where they won't be forgotten. Feed them fortnightly with a liquid fertilizer and repot them if necessary. Most prefer shade, but plants like Christmas cactus (*Schlumbergera*) are best in the sun which will ripen their new shoots and produce lots of flowers.

Softwood cuttings can be taken from many shrubs during early to mid-summer. As their name suggests, the cuttings are taken from soft shoots produced this year.

Remove the top 7.5 cm (3 in), cutting just above a leaf joint. These soft growths dry out very fast, so put them into a polythene bag immediately. For the same reason it's best to do the preparation in a cool shady spot rather than in a hot greenhouse.

With a sharp knife, trim the base of the cutting just below the lowest leaf joint. Remove the lower leaves to leave one pair and the tip of the shoot. If the plant has very large leaves, remove one of the pair to reduce water loss.

Immerse the whole cutting in a solution of fungicide and then dip the base into hormone rooting powder. Dibble it

Softwood cuttings wilt rapidly, so dibble them in quickly, water them with a fungicide and cover with clear polythene. Then put them in a shady place.

into a pot of coir compost mixed 50/50 with vermiculite. You can put a number of cuttings into one pot, depending on its size. Water in with the fungicide solution and cover the pot with thin clear polythene secured with an elastic band to keep in the moisture. Place the pot in a shaded coldframe or outside in a shady place. Most shrubs can be successfully propagated this way. However, if it does fail, have another go with half-ripe cuttings (see page 120).

CHECKLIST

- Plant out vegetables raised under cover like courgettes and sweetcorn.
- Tie in sweet peas and other annual climbers regularly.
- If you run short of salad vegetables, sprout some seeds on the windowsill to fill the gap (see page 33).
- Snap off tomato side shoots as they appear.
- Continue to remove suckers from roses, lilac and other plants before they get too large.
- Apply an extra coat of shading paint to the greenhouse if necessary.
- Finish planting aquatics for a good display this year.
- Early in the month move dwarf peach trees in pots outside – the danger of infection by peach leaf curl has passed.
- Water and ventilate the greenhouse regularly.
- Pinch out the tips of chrysanthemums planted last month.
- Stake gladioli.

JULY

THIS IS A TIME when you'll want to be outside from dawn to dusk. And it's amazing how the garden can change throughout the day. First thing in the morning is, for me, the best time of all. If you can make it outside when the rest of the world's asleep, you'll experience a touch of paradise.

During the day, the sunshine opens all the brightest flowers and when evening falls the perfumed plants really come into their own. Any plant with scented flowers is designed to attract insects, so select a few plants for their smell. What's more, if you do that, you'll never have to spray against pests. I don't.

And at night, go outside with a torch and catch a little of the nightly show. If you've planted things like nicotiana which are heaviest-scented at night, you'll find some fascinating moths you'll never see by day.

◀ *The different shapes and colours of all these herbaceous perennials contrast and combine to create a beautiful tapestry of flowers.*

GARDENS TO VISIT

- **Castle Kennedy Gardens**, Dumfries and Galloway. Landscaped on a grand scale with a huge lily pond, terraces and avenues. Magnificent specimens, particularly the Chilean fire bush (*Embothrium*). Plant centre and refreshments.
- **Great Dixter**, East Sussex. Home of gardener and writer Christopher Lloyd. A glorious plantsman's garden with lots of mixed plants growing informally within a formal structure. Nursery adjoins garden.
- **Levens Hall**, Cumbria. Fantastic clipped specimens of box and yew. Herb gardens and many other attractive borders.
- **Tresco Gardens**, Isles of Scilly, Cornwall. A sub-tropical paradise with plants from around the world. Shrubs reach tree-like proportions in the mild climate. Tea and gift shop.

Looking good

Drought-tolerant plants often prove their worth this month, when long spells of dry weather can really hit the garden hard. While many other plants look limp and exhausted, these relish every bit of baking sun and produce a wonderfully colourful show of flowers and foliage. The key to success is a sunny site and good drainage *all year*, as they detest having to sit in water, especially in winter.

Plants with grey foliage are generally drought-tolerant, like lad's love (*Artemisia*) with silver filigree leaves. Cotton lavender (*Santolina*) also has attractive, finely cut foliage and bears yellow 'buttons' of flowers. *Convolvulus cneorum* has delicate white blooms, *Dorycnium hirsutum* bears clusters of white flowers followed by red berries. Russian sage (*Perovskia*) has tall stems of branched blue flowers. All sages like dry soils, as does rue (*Ruta graveolens*) with its intensely blue leaves. If you have a sensitive skin, though, this one's best avoided since it can cause rashes. *Anthemis tinctoria* 'E.C. Buxton' makes a lovely contrast with masses of lemon-yellow daisy flowers over a long period. Plants with felted woolly leaves like lamb's ears (*Stachys lanata*), *Ballota pseudodictamnus* and *Salvia argentea* are also very resistant to drought.

Sun roses or rock roses love dry sunny conditions and even poor soil. These names generally refer to *Cistus, Halimium*, x *Halimiocistus* and *Helianthemum*. The first three are small to medium shrubs with masses of delicate papery flowers. They're mostly white, but there are a few pink and yellow varieties too. Helianthemums are small spreading plants ideal for rockeries and border edges, and there's a huge range of colours – white, red, orange, cream, yellow and pink.

Plants with succulent, fleshy leaves are also drought-tolerant as they can conserve moisture well. *Sedum spectabile* looks handsome from spring onwards with its clumps of thick, grey-green leaves, and its stems of flower buds that will open shortly.

Yuccas form bold rosettes of large, sharply pointed leaves. They're a dramatic sight in the occasional years when they bear a tall stem laden with creamy-white flowers, but for long-lasting colour it may be better to opt for one with colourful foliage, like *Yucca filamentosa* 'Bright Edge' which is green and gold.

Hardy annuals in borders are really making a spectacular show now. They're so easy and cheap to grow, and there are some gorgeously colourful varieties. Blazing star (*Mentzelia*, formerly *Bartonia*) has golden 'daisy' flowers; *Clarkia* bears pretty double flowers in red, pink, purple and white shades; mallow (*Lavatera*) has large white or deep pink ones; and Californian poppy (*Eschscholzia*) produces delicate flowers of many colours. Sunflowers are speedy growers, popular with children, and birds love the seeds produced by the massive yellow flowers.

Half-hardy annuals need a little more care to grow, but they make an unrivalled show of colour right through summer. Plant them in containers and hanging baskets, group them informally in the gaps in mixed borders, or create complete bedding schemes. There's a huge range of colours from soft pastel shades to gaudy primary colours, so you can plan exactly what you like.

Most people have come across the old favourites, like fiery orange and yellow French and African marigolds, the scarlet poker-like flowers of *Salvia superba*, deep blue *Lobelia*, small pink and white *Begonia semperflorens*, and fluffy blue-mauve *Ageratum*. There are lots of others, including *Mimulus* with red, yellow and orange flowers, which likes a cool shady site, as do busy Lizzies (*Impatiens*) with their red, white and pink blooms. Tobacco plants (*Nicotiana*) with flowers borne on tall stems are particularly good, but if you want perfume go for the pure white ones which give off an exquisite scent in the evening. There's also an unusual shade of lime-green as well as pinks and reds. The 'Domino' varieties are compact and they're especially good in containers. Swan river daisy (*Brachycome*) bears masses of blue, white or pink daisy flowers, and it's also ideal for containers, as is *Nierembergia* 'Mont Blanc' which is smothered in white, golden-eyed flowers. *Mesembryanthemum* (commonly known as 'mezzies' because of their tongue-twisting name!) and *Portulaca* have brightly-coloured flowers in many colours, and fleshy, succulent leaves which indicate that they're sun-lovers and tolerant of dry soils.

Annual climbers with colourful flowers are wonderfully versatile. They can be grown on their own in the usual way up walls and fences, up a tripod of canes or other supports and, because they're not over-vigorous, they can be grown through other plants like shrubs, conifers or climbers. Easiest to grow are climbing nasturtiums with their brightly-coloured red, yellow and orange flowers, and canary creeper (*Tropaeolum peregrinum*) which has prettily-fringed yellow ones. Morning glory (*Ipomoea*) need a little cosseting and a sheltered, sunny site, but it's well worth the effort. The most handsome variety is 'Heavenly Blue' with flowers of an almost unreal shade of deep, clear blue. They open in the morning and are over by evening, though so many flowers are produced they make a near-continual display. There are always lots of new varieties introduced every year, many of which are improved forms of old favourites. Keep a look out for them in garden centres, open gardens and flower shows, as well as in each season's seed catalogues.

Water-garden plants look fabulous in mid-summer. Moisture-loving irises have been flowering for the last month. Look out for *Iris ensata* (formerly *I. kaempferi*) with large, handsome, purple flowers, and the lovely blue-flowered *I. laevigata*. There is a variegated form with striking green- and-white-striped leaves. *I. pseudacorus* 'Variegata' has green and

---

THE GARDEN INDOORS

DRYING AND USING LAVENDER

Lavender isn't just an excellent garden plant. Its wonderfully scented flowers can be dried and used in many different ways indoors.

The flowers are best picked just before they're fully open, early on a fine day and preferably when the dew has dried off. Tie them together in small bunches and hang them to dry in a airy place out of direct sunlight. When the flowers are dry and crisp to the touch, strip them off the stalks. Use lavender in pot-pourri (see page 97) and make little bags of it to slip among piles of linen or clothes.

Lavender 'bottles' make a pretty variation on bags. Pick and dry the flowers and, while the stems are still flexible, tie a small bunch of flowers together just below their heads. Secure a piece of narrow ribbon about 15–20 cm (6–8 in) long in the same place, bend the stems right back over the flowers and weave the ribbon between them so that the flower heads are enclosed in a 'cage' of stems and ribbon. Cut the ribbon and tuck the end in. Trim the stems and add a decorative bow.

For centuries lavender has been used as a natural relaxant. After a hard day hang a muslin bag of dried lavender under the hot tap when you're running a bath and have a long, luxurious, fragrant soak. Then encourage a good night's sleep by tucking a small lavender bag inside your pillow slip.

PLANT OF THE MONTH

Diascias
HEIGHT: 30 cm (1 ft)
SPREAD: 45 cm (1½ ft)
FLOWERING TIME: Summer – autumn
POSITION: Sun
SOIL: Well-drained **HARDY?**: Not reliably

Diascias are long-flowering and versatile little plants that can be used in lots of places around the garden. They have a lax spreading habit that makes them ideal for containers, hanging baskets, rockeries and border edges, particularly when they can spread on to a paved or gravelled path. Spikes of pretty coppery-pink flowers are borne for months on end, often from early summer until the first frosts. The varieties available include 'Ruby Field', 'Salmon Supreme', *Diascia vigilis* and *D. rigescens*.

Diascias can often survive a winter outside, especially if you plant them near a south-facing wall or fence and improve drainage by digging in plenty of coarse grit, though it's best to take cuttings in late summer to over-winter indoors. They'll root very easily and quickly.

gold leaves, and is a much better choice for a garden pond than the green-leaved species, our native flag iris, which is vigorous and not very ornamental.

As the irises fade, water lilies (*Nymphaea*) begin to open their exotic-looking blooms. There's a huge range to choose from, starting with tiny dwarfs that can be grown in a barrel pond, to enormous rampant species that are best suited to a small lake, so it's very important to select one that's the right size for your pond. For the smallest, half-barrel-sized ponds, there are some enchanting water lilies like the 'Laydekeri' hybrids with pink, red and crimson flowers, and the true miniature variety *N. pygmaea* 'Helvola' with tiny, soft yellow flowers. For slightly larger ponds, one of the best water lilies is 'Froebeli' which bears lots of deep, blood-red foliage against dark reddish-green foliage. There are also changeable varieties like 'Sioux', with flowers that open soft yellow flushed with red and gradually change to a pretty coppery-red. For a medium-sized pond, one of the best whites is 'Gonne' or 'Snowball' which bears spectacular, pure white flowers. Don't be tempted to plant the native European white water lily (*N. alba*) as it's extremely vigorous and only suited to very large ponds.

Water lilies are good wildlife plants as they provide shade, shelter and a natural perch. Attract bees and butterflies to the poolside with the tall pink flower spikes of purple loosestrife (*Lythrum salicaria*) and water mint (*Mentha aquatica*) with its mauve powder-puff flowers. Water mint can be invasive with its long, scrambling stems and in a small pond a good alternative would be *Preslia cervina*, which forms a neatly spreading clump of aromatic foliage. Brooklime (*Veronica beccabunga*) bears spikes of blue, white-eyed flowers. In a large bog garden *Eupatorium purpureum* is also wonderful for butterflies with its tall heads of dark pink flowers.

▶ *Frost-tender perennials like these pink marguerites and* Arctotis, *which have larger flowers, just can't be bettered for long-lasting colour.*

General tasks

Conifer hedges can now be trimmed. When you trim the sides, avoid cutting hard back into old brown wood as most conifers rarely regrow if they're cut back too hard. If the hedge is new, don't allow it to get out of hand. Trim the sides as soon as they're wide enough and allow the top to grow 1 m (3 ft) higher than you eventually want it. Then cut back to 15 cm (6 in) lower than needed so that it develops a good bushy top.

Hedges of fast-growing evergreen shrubs like privet and *Lonicera nitida* should be trimmed if they're looking straggly.

Seed can be collected when it's ripe, once the pods have turned brown. Poppies like this Iceland poppy 'Constance Finnis' are easy to grow from seed.

Holidays need a bit of planning so that your garden stays healthy. Arrange for a friend or neighbour to water your plants if possible. Make life easier for them by moving containers and houseplants to a part-shaded place where they won't dry out so quickly, leave the hosepipe uncoiled and watering cans to hand. Just before you go, give everything a good soaking and cut the lawn. Ask someone to harvest sweet peas, runner beans and courgettes (they're normally only too happy to do so!).

Seeds can be collected from herbaceous perennials, shrubs, annuals and other plants when the pods have become brown and dry. Collect seed during dry weather, or spread damp pods on newspaper to dry.

The ripe seeds must first be cleaned. Often they'll just fall out of their capsules; otherwise rub the pods between your hands over a large shallow tray to release the seeds. Pick out the larger pieces of rubbish, then gently blow on the seeds to separate them from the smallest pieces. Most can be sown straight away in pots or trays in the cold-frame. Half-hardy annuals and tender perennials are best stored.

Put the cleaned seed in paper envelopes and label them with the plant name and date. Store them in a cool dry place.

Water should be used economically, especially during long dry periods. Install a water butt to collect rainwater from house, shed and greenhouse roofs. Fit a rainwater-saving device to downpipes to divert water into a butt. Once the butt is full, it'll automatically close up. If the collected water starts to smell, put about 250 g (8 oz) charcoal – the barbecue type is ideal – in the bottom of the barrel.

If you're watering your garden with a hosepipe, do so early in the morning or in the evening, to prevent losing too much by evaporation.

Ornamental garden

BULBS AND TUBERS

Autumn-flowering bulbs can be planted now to make a gorgeous show of colour in September and October. Their flowers rise straight out of the ground by themselves, because their leaves have died back by early summer.

Autumn crocuses have delicate typical crocus flowers, but don't confuse them with *Colchicums*. The 'real' crocuses are those like *Crocus speciosus* which has beautiful blue flowers and *Crocus zonatus* with lilac-pink ones. However, *Colchicums* are also called 'autumn crocus' and are very different. They have pink or purple flowers and they're ideal for planting in grass or underneath shrubs and trees. The flower stems are weak, so support them by growing them through other low-growing plants.

Nerine bowdenii should be planted against a south-facing wall: they like a sunny position. These bear bright pink flowers on tall stems.

Hardy cyclamen produce lovely dark pink flowers on short stems. They're tolerant plants which can be grown in dry inhospitable places such as under mature trees. Don't buy tubers, which are normally too dry to survive and are often also harvested illegally, mainly from countries like Turkey where wild populations are now threatened. Buy them in pots instead, or wait until autumn when they're in flower and you can see exactly what you're getting.

Bulbs that were moved to trenches to die back should now be lifted, and stored in boxes or trays in a cool dry place. Rub off the dead leaves and skins, inspect the bulbs carefully and throw out any with signs of rot or damage.

CLIMBERS

Air layering is a good way to propagate some climbers if the shoots are way off the ground. Plants like *Clematis* and

---

FERTILIZERS

Fertilizers are concentrated plant foods, and they're important for a successful garden as it's inevitable that more nutrients are taken from the soil than go back in naturally.

Fertilizers roughly divide into main groups; artificial and organic. Artificial ones are quite concentrated, so they must be applied with reasonable precision and kept off the plant foliage. There is evidence that they damage soil organisms and inhibit the bacteria that naturally produce nitrogen. Organic fertilizers have no adverse effects, and there's no need to be exact in their application. Organic ones are easily distinguished by their contents which are usually reflected by their name; fish, blood and bone, chicken manure concentrate and bone meal. The three major nutrients are nitrogen, phosphorus and potassium (known by the symbols N, P and K respectively). Nitrogen is used for leaf and stem growth, phosphorus for roots and potassium (often referred to as potash) for flowers and fruit. For most garden uses a compound fertilizer, which is a mixture of these three elements, is sufficient. The packet will carry details of the balance of elements it contains, expressed as a ratio. For example, 5:7:10 means 5 parts of nitrogen, 7 of phosphate and 10 of potassium or potash.

Depending on the time of year, the balance of the fertilizer used should vary. For example, plants need more nitrogen in spring and summer, whereas in autumn they need more phosphorus to promote root growth.

Controlled-release fertilizers are particularly useful, as they only need to be applied once or twice in a season. These are artificial fertilizers which are pelleted and coated with resin which dissolves over a long period to gradually make the nutrients available to the plants.

▶ *Containers need frequent watering, usually once a day, especially if they're crammed as full as this one.*

Akebia can be difficult to layer in the usual way, so you have to take the mountain to Mohammed.

Select a healthy stem and remove a sliver of bark just below a leaf joint, using a sharp knife. Wrap a handful of moist sphagnum moss round the joint and then surround it with clear polythene. Tie it at the top and bottom to hold it in place. When a reasonable amount of root has formed, usually in a couple of months, cut the layer from its parent and pot it up. Put it in a coldframe or a sheltered spot to grow on for planting out next spring or summer.

Wisteria should now be pruned. All the young whippy side shoots produced this year should be shortened to within five or six buds of the main stem.

WATER EFFICIENCY

Water can start to become short at this time, so guard against hosepipe bans. Collect water from the roof in a butt and, if you live in a dry area, you could even link two or three butts together to increase capacity. All you need is a sort of overflow system with a pipe from just below the top of the first butt to the top of the second.

Mulch the borders with compost, manure, shredded prunings – anything organic. You have only to lift a stone to see how much moisture is retained where evaporation is prevented.

In the kitchen garden, mulch between rows with black polythene or even a few sheets of newspaper covered with a sprinkling of soil to hide it and hold it down. This also prevents weed growth, of course, which would otherwise compete for water.

When you do water, reserve precious supplies for demanding plants like fruiting vegetables and shallow-rooted ornamentals. The annuals will be particularly at risk, for example, while shrubs, unless they're newly planted, will survive longer.

Give plants a really good soaking when you do water. Simply sprinkling the surface brings roots to the top where they're even more vulnerable.

Best of all, install a 'leaky-pipe' system. This is a porous pipe which gently seeps water just where it's wanted, avoiding wasteful splashing.

TAKING HALF-RIPE CUTTINGS

Half-ripe cuttings are taken from this year's shoots when the stem has just started to become woody.

1 *Take cuttings about 10 cm (4 in) long, either from the end part of the shoot or by gently pulling off side shoots to remove a small sliver of bark from the main stem. Trim the heel of bark or cut stems just below a leaf joint.*

2 *Take off the leaves on the bottom two-thirds of each cutting, and remove the tip if the growth is very soft. Dip the whole cutting in a solution of fungicide and the base into hormone rooting powder.*

3 *Then either put the cuttings into pots of coir compost mixed with equal parts of vermiculite, or line them out in a coldframe in soil to which sharp sand has been added.*

Regular care of container plants is essential if they are to continue giving a top-class display right through the summer. By now the plants will have grown to fill the containers so they'll need lots of water, usually once a day and sometimes more, especially if there's a hot, drying wind. Hanging baskets dry out even faster as there's air movement all round them.

Unless you've added a controlled-release fertilizer to the compost, all containers will need to be fed with a liquid fertilizer twice a week. A high potash type is best, such as tomato fertilizer.

Deadheading flowering plants as soon as the flowers have died will pay dividends as it encourages them to produce lots more blooms. Simply pinch the dead flower heads off, once or twice a week.

HERBACEOUS PERENNIALS

Perennials that have flowered like oriental poppies and herbaceous geraniums should be cut back to ground level to encourage new growth and a possible second flush of flowers. Tall perennials like delphiniums should just have the top of the flowered stem removed to encourage new flowering side shoots, though this is really feasible only in warmer areas. Peonies should have only their dead flowers removed as their leaves need to die back naturally.

ROSES

Diseases like blackspot and rust can often take hold in summer, particularly after long spells of damp weather. Reduce the spread of disease by gathering and disposing of all infected leaves that fall to the ground.

Rust is more likely to attack potash-deficient plants, so regular feeding with rose fertilizer helps prevent it. Spraying with Myclobutanil every two weeks helps control rust if it appears. See page 62 for treatment of blackspot.

Powdery mildew is encouraged by spells of hot dry weather, and it's more likely to attack plants that are under stress because of a shortage of food and water. Spray every two weeks with

Fish can become very stressed due to lack of oxygen in hot, sultry weather, so spray the surface of the pond with water from a hosepipe to introduce oxygen.

sulphur if the attack is extremely severe.

Some roses are more liable to infection than others. Certain varieties that are regularly attacked may be best replaced with ones that have some natural resistance. Check in a good rose book before buying to see which varieties are best.

SHRUBS

Half-ripe cuttings are an easy way of propagating many shrubs from now until early autumn.

When the cuttings have rooted, either in late summer or next spring, pot them individually and grow the young plants on until they're well established, when they can be planted out.

WATER GARDEN

Hot weather causes loss of water by evaporation, so top up the pond during long dry spells. Rainwater is best, but tap water can be added little and often so as not to upset the pond's balance.

Keep an eye on your fish. If they're gulping for air close to the surface, there's not enough oxygen in the water

and they could even die in extreme cases. To relieve them temporarily, spray the pond with a jet of water from a hose. If it happens often, it's worth installing a small fountain so that the splashing water can constantly replenish the oxygen in the pond.

Oxygenating plants should be thinned if they've produced an abundance of growth. Cut off the surplus with secateurs if it's easily reached, or use a rake to pull it out. Leave the trimmings piled by the pond for a couple of days so that any creatures hiding inside can return to the water. Remove any blanketweed as it appears.

Pests like greenfly occasionally attack water lilies and marginal plants. Of course, chemicals should never be used on pond plants as they'll poison the water and any fish, but a safe and easy method of control is to weight the leaves to push them under water for a day or two, where fish and other creatures can feast on the pests.

Kitchen garden

FRUIT

Strawberries should have all their old leaves cut off after harvesting has finished. Rake off and compost the old leaves and straw, and pull up any weeds.

Summer-fruiting raspberries should be pruned after harvest: cut all the old fruited canes down to the ground. Repair or tighten the training wires if necessary, then tie the new canes in about 10 cm (4 in) apart. Cut out weak spindly canes and bodily pull up any which have grown between the rows. This deters them from regrowing.

VEGETABLES

Autumn and winter salad vegetables can be sown now. Claytonia or winter purslane does best on a sandy soil, cornsalad or lamb's lettuce and rocket are happy in most situations, and land cress likes a rich, fairly moist soil. Some of the oriental vegetables (see page 124) are also useful in salads. Sow seed thinly in rows 23 cm (9 in) apart. With the exception of land cress, all these plants can either be grown as a cut-and-come-again crop where the seedlings are left to grow densely, or thinned to around 10 cm (4 in) apart and the plants harvested individually.

Salad onions can be sown thinly to over-winter for harvesting in early spring. A final sowing of beetroot can be made in mild areas.

After harvesting the fruit, cut back all the strawberry foliage with shears and rake it off.

Sow lettuce in rows, or in trays if the weather is hot (see page 108). Prick out seedlings sown in trays last month and plant them out when two adult leaves are well developed.

Celery growing in trenches should be earthed up when the plants are about 30 cm (1 ft) high, so that the stems become white and succulent. Use a draw hoe to pull soil up around the plants, or tie brown paper collars around each plant so that only the top third is left exposed.

Diseases that can attack vegetables in summer include blight which attacks potatoes and tomatoes. Yellowish-brown patches appear on the leaves and these eventually turn black and die. White fungal strands grow on the leaf undersides. Cut back and burn the top growth on potatoes and destroy entire tomato

Ornamental cabbages look wonderful in containers with flowering plants like nasturtiums. Nasturtium leaves and flowers make a lovely tangy addition to salads.

plants. Unaffected plants should be sprayed with copper fungicide and again two weeks later, which may prevent the disease spreading. Potatoes should be dug up and used as soon as possible, though affected tubers may be discoloured with brown marks.

Clubroot is a serious disease that attacks members of the cabbage family. There's no cure and it'll remain in the soil more or less forever. The leaves of affected plants become discoloured and wilt, and the roots are distorted and swollen. The effects of the disease can be mitigated by improving drainage and liming a piece of ground especially for brassicas to around pH level 7.0. One solution is to start plants off in 10-cm (4-in) pots and put them out once a good rootball has formed. They'll still get affected but the healthy start will ensure a harvestable crop.

Downy mildew and grey mould (*Botrytis*) can often be prevented by spacing plants well apart so that there's plenty of air movement.

Virus diseases cause stunted growth and mottled foliage. There's no cure, so remove and burn affected leaves.

Endive should be blanched to prevent it becoming bitter-flavoured and to make the foliage white and more palatable. When the plants are three months old, cover each one with a flower pot that's had its drainage hole blocked to ensure that the plant's in total darkness. They're normally ready to harvest after about ten days.

Endive can also be sown for an autumn crop in rows 30 cm (1 ft) apart..

Harvest vegetables as soon as they become ready, for the best flavour. Cut courgettes and pick beans regularly to encourage more to form. Globe artichokes are best harvested when the heads are plump but before the scales start to open; cut the heads with a small portion of stem attached.

Onions, garlic and shallots are ready to harvest when the leaves start to turn yellow and the tops bend over. Loosen the roots with a fork and leave them for a week or so. Then lift the crop, shake off the soil and leave the bulbs out in the sun to dry fully. Ideally spread them out on a wire netting 'table' just off the ground so that the air circulates fully around them. If it starts raining, cover the bulbs with polythene or bring them into a greenhouse or shed to finish drying.

Store shallots in mesh bags, old tights or boxes in a dry frost-free place. Onions and garlic can also be put in bags, or plaited into ropes.

Oriental vegetables can be sown now. Most varieties have attractive leaves, so they can be sown in short rows or patches in ornamental borders as well as in the vegetable garden. Sow Chinese radish, mizuna greens, mustard greens, kai-choi (green-in-the-snow) and spinach mustard in rows 30 cm (1 ft) apart and thin to 15–30 cm (6–12in) between plants. The smaller spacing gives smaller plants for an earlier harvest. Mizuna and mustard greens can also be grown as a cut-and-come-again seedling crop. Sow pak choi and Chinese cabbage in rows 30 cm (1 ft) apart. Put three seeds per station 23 cm (9 in) apart in the rows and thin to one seedling.

Vegetables to sow now also include beetroot, Florence fennel, Swiss chard, radicchio (leaf chicory) and turnips. In a seedbed sow spring cabbage around the middle of the month in colder areas, but delay until early August in mild areas.

If there's no space available for direct sowing because crops haven't quite matured, sow seed in pots or modules so that the new plants can be put in as soon as there's room.

Water vegetables during dry weather, particularly newly transplanted ones and plants that produce pods or fruits like courgettes, runner beans and peas. If sowing seed, take out the drill, mix in a little coir compost which helps retain moisture, and water the drill well before sowing.

Greenhouse and windowsill

Greenhouse vegetables like aubergines, peppers and tomatoes should be fed twice weekly with liquid tomato fertilizer and watered whenever necessary, usually daily. Continue to snap off tomato side shoots and wind plants round their supporting strings. Stake and tie other plants.

Ventilate the greenhouse all day, and during the night too if the weather's hot. Damp down paths frequently.

Standards of plants like fuchsias can be trained from rooted cuttings over a cou-ple of years. Select strong, straight, healthy cuttings and leave the top intact so that it grows upwards in a single shoot. Support it with a split cane or a small bamboo one. Pinch off any side shoots as they appear and start removing a few lower leaves when the plant is about 15 cm (6 in) high. Lantanas can be trained in the same way to make attractive and unusual standards.

Shrubs can also be grown as standards. Evergreen varieties like golden privet (*Ligustrum ovalifolium* 'Aureum'), *Berberis* and *Elaeagnus pungens* 'Maculata' look particularly good in pots for an unusual patio display.

Water and ventilate the greenhouse regularly. The vents can now be left half-open at night unless the weather's cold, and both the vents and the door should be fully open on sunny days. If you're out at work all day, it may be well worth fitting an automatic vent opener.

Damp down the greenhouse on hot days by sprinkling the paths and benches with water. This keeps the atmosphere humid and stops the plants drying out too quickly.

CHECKLIST

- Put out a large shallow dish of water for birds and hedgehogs if the weather's dry.
- Dead-head all plants frequently, especially roses, annuals and tender perennials.
- Layer border carnations by pegging down the tips.
- Disbud dahlias and chrysanthemums by removing all but the very top bud if you want large flowers for cutting.
- Cut back straggly violas to encourage new shoots for cuttings.
- Continue pruning deciduous shrubs that have flowered (see page 105).
- Pinch out runner beans when they've reached the top of the supports.
- Pinch out the tops of outdoor tomatoes once three flower trusses have formed.
- Plant out members of the cabbage family sown earlier in a seedbed.
- Harvest herbs for drying and storing (see page 163).
- Sow parsley for winter use.
- Water new lawns thoroughly during dry weather.
- Check lilies regularly for lily beetle (see page 102).
- Order daffodil and narcissus bulbs.

Aubergines and other greenhouse vegetables need regular watering, usually at least once a day, now they've formed large plants.

AUGUST

THERE'S NEVER REALLY a good time to leave the garden to its own devices but August is as good as any to take a holiday. Before you go, cut the lawn, get the weeding done and water as much as you can. Harvest all the vegetables available and instruct your neighbours to come and pick things like runner beans. They'll stop producing if they're left, but continued harvesting will keep them cropping. It's a good way to repay the favour of watering and so on too.

Put your houseplants on a towel in the bath with the end of the towel dipped into a bucket of water and draw the curtains. If you can't get neighbourly help, you can now buy cheap automatic watering for garden and greenhouse.

◀ *The tall coral-pink plumes of* Macleaya cordata *make a splendid backdrop to clumps of bright pink and red phlox, while the lime-yellow flowers of lady's mantle tumble onto the gravel path.*

GARDENS TO VISIT

- **Beth Chatto Gardens**, Essex. Well-known plantswoman and writer Beth Chatto has created an inspirational garden on a difficult site. In August herbaceous plants and ornamental grasses look at their best. Plants for sale.
- **Crathes Castle**, Grampian. Walled gardens contain eight themed gardens. Herbaceous borders are especially good with many unusual plants. Wild gardens. Restaurant, shop and plants for sale.
- **Holker Hall and Gardens**, Cumbria. Magnificent formal and woodland gardens. Magnolias, rhododendrons and azaleas in spring. Roses in summer. Many rare trees and shrubs. Spectacular water features. Shop, café, plants for sale.
- **Powis Castle**, Powys. Steep terraces have a mild microclimate where many less hardy plants are grown. Old containers planted up for superb summer colour. Many fine climbers. Large wild garden. Café, plants for sale.

Looking good

Tender perennials are a relatively new and exciting group of plants that make a tremendous display of colour right through the summer. They can be used in tubs, borders and hanging baskets. Most are sun-lovers so they do best in a warm sunny spot with well-drained soil.

There are many tempting plants with an enormous range of flower shapes and colours as well as distinctive foliage. They vary from 15 cm to 1 m (6 in to 3 ft) in height. A number of varieties have colourful daisy-like flowers and, just to confuse you, the name 'African daisy' refers to *Arctotis, Euryops, Felicia, Gazania* and *Osteospermum*.

Osteospermums include upright varieties like the handsome creamy-yellow 'Buttermilk', and 'Whirligig' with unusual quill-shaped white petals. If you want trailing ones, look for 'Cannington Roy' (purple-pink), 'Tresco Purple' (dark purple) and 'Silver Sparkler' (white flowers, variegated leaves).

Gazanias are low-growing and compact, which makes them particularly good for containers. The more vivid oranges and yellows tend to take centre stage, but there are some lovely softer shades like 'Cream Dream' with pale yellow flowers and silvery foliage. *Arctotis* (also known as *Venidio*) have larger, even more exotic and brightly coloured flowers that pack a real punch, like 'Flame' with stunning orange-red blooms.

Argyranthemums (marguerites) form large, woody bushes and come in several colours. There are single-flowered forms with simple, pretty, daisy flowers, like 'Jamaica Primrose' (pale yellow), 'Peach Cheeks' (pale peach) and 'Royal Haze' (white with silver foliage). The double-flowered ones like 'Vancouver' (deep pink) look like little pompons.

As well as these larger groups of plants, there are loads of others well worth trying. *Felicia amelloides* provides the best blue of all, with lots of miniature, cool blue flowers with a little yellow eye. It forms a tiny bush, whereas *Euryops pectinatus* makes a much taller, rather woody plant with masses of bright yellow flowers and finely cut grey-green foliage. *Nemesia fruticans* has spikes of mauve flowers and 'Confetti' is a pretty, soft pink. *Cosmos atrosanguineus* has little, dahlia-like, deep velvety-red flowers that have a delicious scent of dark chocolate. Some of the less hardy *Salvias* can be grown from seed, like *S. patens* 'Cambridge Blue' with exquisite, deep blue flowers, and *S. microphylla* with red ones. New tender perennials are coming on the market all the time, so keep an eye on what's available.

All these plants will be killed by frost unless you're in a very mild area, but don't let that put you off. They'll need to be brought into a heated greenhouse or indoors for the winter or, since most can be grown easily from cuttings taken in late summer (see page 132), they can easily be over-wintered on a windowsill indoors.

Butterflies flock to nectar-rich flowers, particularly in July and August. Frequent garden visitors usually include the comma, peacock, red admiral and small tortoiseshell. Not all garden flowers are suitable for butterflies to feed on, so plant some of their favourites.

Top of the list has to be the aptly named butterfly bush (*Buddleia davidii*) with its masses of colourful cone-shaped flowers in many colours – white, pale blue, pink, purple and violet. 'Harlequin' and 'Masquerade' have variegated leaves and reddish-purple flowers. Buddleias are easy to grow and quickly form large bushes, though they can be hard pruned in early spring to keep them small. Other good butterfly shrubs include *Hebe*, hyssop, lavender and privet.

Summer- and autumn-flowering herbaceous perennials popular with butterflies include Michaelmas daisies (*Aster*), catmint (*Nepeta*), ice plant (*Sedum spectabile*) and scabious. *Clematis heracleifolia* is a handsome and unusual herbaceous plant that produces 90-cm (3-ft) stems of clustered blue flowers which have a wonderful hyacinth-like scent. See page 58 for annual flowers to attract butterflies.

Plants with colourful foliage can come into their own in high summer when many flowering plants have finished. Purple foliage looks exceptionally handsome, but take care not to overdo it as a little bold colour can go a long way. The smoke bush (*Cotinus*) is an easily grown large shrub. 'Royal Purple' has deep purple leaves and 'Grace' is a softer purplish-red with really big leaves. Several *Berberis thunbergii* varieties like 'Red Chief' and 'Dart's Red Lady' have reddish-purple leaves. Japanese maples (*Acer palmatum* varieties) are extremely lovely shrubs or small trees with delicately cut leaves, though they need a moist, well-drained, acid soil and a sheltered site in dappled shade in order to thrive. There are many different varieties with subtle differences in foliage and colour, so it's best to view a selection before deciding which one to buy.

Golden foliage isn't as overpowering as purple, though it still needs to be used with a little caution. The golden Indian bean tree (*Catalpa bignonioides* 'Aurea') looks best as a single specimen where its large, greenish-gold leaves can be fully appreciated. If you prune it hard each year you'll get the brightest foliage and keep it small. Plant it in a sheltered spot. Golden cut-leaved elder (*Sambucus racemosa* 'Plumosa Aurea') has attractive, finely cut, golden leaves, and again should be pruned hard in early spring. Golden dogwood (*Cornus alba* 'Aurea'), *Physocarpus opulifolius* 'Luteus' and *Philadelphus coronarius* 'Aureus' are all easily grown shrubs with handsome greenish-gold leaves. Golden foliage can be scorched by bright sunlight, so plant these shrubs in light shade.

All these purple- and gold-foliaged shrubs are deciduous. See page 176 for evergreens with colourful foliage.

THE GARDEN INDOORS

DRYING FLOWERS FOR ARRANGEMENTS

It's not hard to save some of the garden's summer colour to brighten up your house through the winter. Many flowers and seed heads can easily be preserved by drying and, if you like flower arranging, they can be combined into pretty, long-lasting decorations.

Lots of annuals and perennials make particularly good dried flowers. Annuals include *Acroclinium*, bells of Ireland (*Molucella*), *Gomphrena*, *Helichrysum* and larkspur. Perennials include *Achillea*, baby's breath (*Gypsophila*), Cupid's dart (*Catananche*), globe thistle (*Echinops*), masterwort (*Astrantia*) and sea lavender (*Limonium*). Ornamental grasses, both annual and perennial (see pages 58 and 140), have a variety of very attractive flower heads.

Pick the flowers just before they're fully open, on a sunny day after the dew has dried. Tie them together in small bunches with soft string or twine. Hang them upside-down in a dry airy room with little or no direct sunlight, but never in the kitchen or bathroom where the atmosphere is damp. Leave them until the flowers are dry and crisp to the touch.

The colours of thin-petalled flowers like delphiniums can easily fade, though it can often be retained by drying them more quickly. Hang them upside-down in the airing cupboard until the petals are dry. Grasses with fluffy flower heads are best dried upright, standing in empty containers.

Some seed heads can burst or deteriorate after drying, like those of reed-maces (bulrushes) and gladwyn iris (*Iris foetidissima*). Spray them with clear varnish or hair lacquer as soon as they're dry.

General tasks

The pretty lemon-yellow 'pokers' of Kniphofia *'Little Maid' are perfect with the flat, reddish heads of* Sedum spectabile *'Brilliant'.*

Deep beds are an excellent way to grow vegetables if your ground is heavy and likely to become waterlogged. Summer is a good time to make such beds, rather than later in the year when the soil is hard to dig.

Mark out beds 1.2 m (4 ft) wide, separated by permanent paths which could be either paved or gravelled. For a really smart appearance you could edge the beds with boards. Double dig the beds, mixing in plenty of well-rotted organic matter, and from then on you do all the work from the side paths and never stand on the soil, except to single dig each winter. The drainage and fertility are

improved and there's no problem with soil compaction. Deep beds are also very easy to cover with clear polythene or cloches for a very early start in spring.

Deadheading and harvesting is best done a couple of times a week to get the most from your plants. Leaving dead heads on flowering plants will make them think that they've done their work for the season, and the same goes for vegetables, especially summer beans.

PLANT OF THE MONTH

Blue spiraea *(Caryopteris x clandonensis).*
HEIGHT: 1–1.2 m (3–4 ft)
SPREAD: 60 cm–1m (2–3 ft)
FLOWERING TIME: July–September
POSITION: Sun
SOIL: Preferably well-drained **HARDY?**: Yes

This easily grown shrub is a mass of beautiful blue flowers in high summer. It's suitable for the smallest garden, forming a neat mound of grey-green aromatic leaves. Bees love the clusters of spiky flowers, which are borne all along its branches, making the whole plant a haze of blue.

Named varieties are best as their flowers are slightly deeper in colour. Choose from 'Arthur Simmonds', 'Heavenly Blue' and 'Kew Blue'. A new variety, 'Worcester Gold', has pretty greenish-gold leaves that contrast well with the flowers. Propagate by softwood cuttings in June.

Ornamental garden

ANNUALS, BIENNIALS AND TENDER PERENNIALS

Annuals that have finished flowering can be pulled up and composted. It's useful to have some standby plants in pots – perhaps some more annuals in flower or other plants like dahlias – so that they can be planted into the gaps. Alternatively, transplant biennials like wallflowers from their nursery bed. The extra growing time will make them into bumper plants to flower next spring.

GROW YOUR OWN PERENNIALS

Collecting and sowing seeds from your own herbaceous perennials is not only fascinating, it's more successful than buying it. Fresh seed will nearly always germinate much better than if it's been stored.

You need to try to get the seed just before it falls, so keep an eye on the plants. When the seed capsules turn brown and dry, they're ready. Choose a dry day and carefully cut the heads and invert them into a paper bag. Take the bags back to the house or shed and tip them out on to newspaper. Often the seed will have come out cleanly, but if it doesn't, make sure that you sort out and throw away the chaff since it's here that fungus disease lurks.

Sow the seeds immediately on the surface of coir compost. Cover with horticultural vermiculite and put the trays into a coldframe. When you've done them all, cover with a piece of thin clear polythene and keep an eye on them so that it can be removed as soon as the first seedling shows. With many perennials that may not be until the following spring, so be patient.

Containers and hanging baskets should still be fed twice a week to maintain a really good display. This month it's best to switch to a high-nitrogen liquid feed that will give plants a boost for the rest of the season. If controlled-release fertilizer was used it may now be exhausted, so containers will also benefit from liquid feeding.

Take off dead flowers regularly to prolong flowering and, of course, never let containers go short of water.

Tender perennials, including fuchsias and geraniums, can be easily propagated by cuttings taken in late summer and early autumn. Select healthy, strong, non-flowering shoots and take off about 10 cm (4 in) of the tip. With a sharp knife, trim the base just below a leaf joint and remove the leaves on the bottom half of the cutting. In the case of geraniums, take off the 'stipules', or little flaps of tissue below the leaves. Dip the base in hormone powder and dibble it into a pot of coconut-fibre compost. Cover fuchsias with clear polythene and put them in a shaded coldframe or on a windowsill out of direct sunlight. Geraniums are best left uncovered on the greenhouse staging or in the frame.

BULBS

Daffodils and narcissi are best planted before the end of September. Larger varieties are ideal for naturalizing in grass or for grouping informally in borders. Dwarf varieties are best planted in tubs, raised beds or rockeries so that their delicate flowers can be fully appreciated. They all look best if they're planted in natural-looking clumps and drifts, rather than in straight rows, so set the bulbs out on the ground first to be sure that they're in the right place. It may sound obvious, but put bulbs in last if you're planting up a new border.

Planting at the right depth is important because shallow planting leads to non-flowering. As a guide, the planting hole should be three times the depth of the bulb, so a 5-cm (2-in) bulb should be covered with 10 cm (4 in) of soil. Err on the deep side if anything. A special bulb planter is the easiest method of planting. On heavy soil or where there's any danger of the ground becoming waterlogged, put a layer of coarse grit in the planting hole first to keep the vulnerable base plate dry and free from rotting.

If the ground isn't ready, or if you're not sure where to plant, pot up the bulbs instead so that you'll be able to put them exactly where they're needed in spring. Take care to plant deeply enough. Lift and replant old congested clumps of daffodils and narcissi, as over-crowded ones won't flower so freely. Generally this is best done every five to six years.

Early spring-flowering bulbs like the windflower (*Anemone blanda*) are best planted as soon as possible. Plant them 2.5 cm (1 in) deep in natural-looking groups or drifts. Snowdrops (*Galanthus*), winter aconites (*Eranthis hyemalis*) and cyclamen should not be planted now since dry bulbs often give disappointing results: in these instances planting flowered bulbs in spring is much more reliable (see page 23).

Herbaceous Perennials

Carnations and pinks can be propagated by layering. Select healthy, vigorous, young shoots and peg them down into pots of compost or directly on to the soil, securing them with wire bent into a hairpin shape. They'll normally root within a few weeks.

Cut back perennials that have spread and flopped over, like *Artemisia* 'Silver Queen' or *Achillea*. Prune the stems back to the ground, feed with a general fertilizer, and in a couple of weeks the plant will produce a mound of fresh foliage. Do the same to hardy geraniums if they weren't cut back earlier. Thin out the stems of *Anthemis* to encourage basal growth.

If you don't want the seed, dead-head all perennials to encourage more flowers.

Roses

Diseased leaves that have fallen to the ground are best gathered and disposed of regularly as the disease spores can over-winter in the soil. Burn the leaves or put them in the dustbin.

Watch out for rust, mildew and black-spot. See pages 62 and 120 for treatment.

New roses are best planted in autumn, but now is a good time to visit specialist nurseries, flowers shows and display gardens to see different ones in flower. Order early as new introductions and less usual varieties sell out fast.

Ramblers should be pruned after they've flowered, but climbers are best left until spring. Cut out the shoots which have flowered, removing them as near to the ground as possible, then tie the new ones in their place. A pruning saw may be needed to tackle thicker branches. If not many new shoots have been produced, leave a few of the old ones but cut their side shoots back to two or three buds.

Mature ramblers produce lots of long, whippy, thorn-laden branches several metres long, so it's wise to gear up before tackling them! As well as thornproof gloves and stout clothes, wear a pair of safety goggles to protect your eyes. Plastic ones don't cost much and they could save you from an injury.

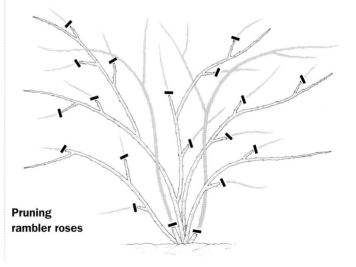

Pruning rambler roses

Keep lavender bushes in shape by lightly trimming the whole plant once it has flowered.

SHRUBS

Camellias can suffer from bud drop before flowering in spring. The most usual cause is lack of water now, when the buds are just beginning to form. Most susceptible are plants that are growing against walls or fences where the ground tends to be dry. Make sure that they don't dry out for long periods, and improve poor soils by adding a couple of buckets of garden compost.

Half-ripe cuttings can still be taken from most shrubs. It's especially worth propagating those which could be killed in a severe winter, like Californian lilac (*Ceanothus*), sun rose (*Cistus*), *Fuchsia*, *Hebe*, myrtle, daisy bush (*Olearia*) and wall germander (*Teucrium*).

Lavender, cotton lavender (*Santolina*) and curry plant (*Helichrysum serotinum*) should be trimmed lightly after flowering using shears. Lavender can be easily raised from cuttings. Select non-flowering side shoots about 7.5 cm (3 in) long and gently pull them from the main stem. Trim the heel of bark with a knife and take off the leaves on the bottom two-thirds of the shoot. Line out the cuttings in sandy soil in a coldframe, or put them in pots.

Kitchen garden

FRUIT

Summer-prune trained fruit trees:
Cordon apples and pears. Side shoots growing from the main stem should be cut back to 7.5 cm (3 in). Those shoots pruned this way last year will have produced smaller side shoots, which should be cut back to 2.5 cm (1 in). This encourages the formation of short fruit-bearing spurs for next year.

Once the cordon tree has reached its desired height, treat the top or leading shoot as above.

Espalier and fan-trained trees. Sideshoots growing from the main branches should be pruned as for cordons (above).

Fan-trained acid cherries, nectarines and peaches. New shoots growing from the main branches should be shortened to 10 cm (4 in), and side shoots which are produced from these should be pruned to 5 cm (2 in).

Fan-trained plums and sweet cherries. After harvest, shorten by half all the shoots that have borne fruit.

Bush cherries and plums should be pruned after they've fruited. First take out any dead and damaged branches, and any rubbing or crossing ones. Then, if the branches are still over-crowded, thin them out to let light and air through the tree. This helps the wood to ripen and prevents disease problems. Try to make as few cuts as possible, especially with plums, as they're prone to disease.

Strawberry runners can be potted up into 18-cm (7-in) pots and left outside, ready for forcing in winter to produce an early crop next year. If your greenhouse is likely to be packed in spring (most are!), pot them into hanging baskets which are easier to squeeze in. Alternatively, you can now buy small growing bags for strawberries.

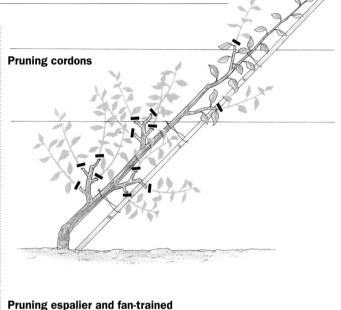

Pruning cordons

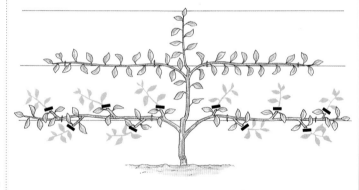

Pruning espalier and fan-trained apples and pears

Pruning fan-trained acid cherries, nectarines and peaches

HERBS

Half-ripe cuttings can be taken of shrubby herbs like bay, hyssop, rosemary, rue and sage (see page 120). Put the cuttings individually into 7.5-cm (3-in) pots and keep them in the greenhouse or on a cool windowsill over winter.

Parsley is often used in large quantities all year round. For a winter supply, sow a row or two of seed outside or put out young plants, for covering with cloches in October.

Pot up a few of your favourite herbs, so that they can be moved inside in October to provide a regular winter supply. Plants like mint and lemon balm can be dug up from the garden. Parsley is best grown fresh from seed. Select young plants of shrubby herbs like sage and rosemary – those raised from cuttings last year are ideal (see above).

VEGETABLES

Carrots benefit from protection against the second generation of carrot flies that appear this month. The most effective control is to cover the entire crop with horticultural fleece.

Marrows, pumpkins and squashes can be rested on pieces of wood or poly-thene while they ripen. Fruits sitting on the ground can rot or suffer slug attack, especially during wet weather.

Sow a final outdoor crop of carrots, lettuce, radish and spinach beet. If the weather's hot, see page 108 for tips on sowing lettuce. Salad onions can be sown until early September for harvesting in early spring (see page 70 for spacings). Onions specially bred for over-wintering like 'Express Yellow' can be sown now for June and July harvest. Sow the seeds 2.5 cm (1 in) apart in rows 30 cm (1 ft) apart. Timing is important – it should be around the middle of the month if you live in the north, but later the further the south you are, the end of August being the latest.

Tomatoes growing outside can have their tops pinched out when three trusses of fruit have formed, to encourage them to develop and ripen fully before the end of the season. Continue snapping off side shoots as they appear. (This does not apply to bush tomatoes.)

Virus diseases often become apparent in late summer. Watch out for yellow mottling on leaves, especially of courgettes, cucumbers and tomatoes. Pull up and destroy infected plants.

After harvesting and drying onions (see page 124), plait or tie the long stems together to form attractive ropes. Remember to rub off the dirty outer skins first.

Greenhouse and windowsill

Cyclamen that were rested earlier in the year can now be started into growth. They can also be grown from seed. Sow at 15–18°C (60–65°F) in seedtrays and transplant the seedlings when they're large enough to handle.

Greenhouse heaters should be cleaned, checked and overhauled. Winter seems a long way off, but it could take a few weeks to get your heater repaired if it needs attention.

CHECKLIST

- Stop feeding roses, and shrubs in containers, as it'll encourage soft growth that will be prone to frost damage.
- Complete summer-pruning of wisterias.
- Propagate rhododendrons by layering.
- Finish trimming conifer and evergreen shrub hedges.
- Maintain ponds (see page 106). Thin out over-crowded water lily leaves.
- Start preparing ground for seeding new lawns next month (see page 25).
- Pot hyacinths for Christmas flowering indoors (see page 141).
- Sow Browallia, Calceolaria and poor man's orchid (Schizanthus) in the greenhouse for pot plants (see page 21).
- Prune summer-fruiting raspberries, taking out fruited canes and tying in new ones 10 cm (4 in) apart.
- Prop up heavily laden branches of fruit trees.
- Prune side shoots on gooseberry cordons to within 2.5 cm (1 in) of the old wood.
- Cut and dry herbs for winter (see page 163).
- Earth up or wrap blanching varieties of celery.
- Lift, dry and store onions and garlic.

POTTING CYCLAMEN

Cyclamen can be kept from year to year, and they make bigger and better plants every season. Those from last year that have been resting during the summer can now be started into growth.

1 *Gently remove the tuber and compost from its old pot and rub off the old compost. If the tuber hasn't outgrown the pot, leave it in but remove the top third of the the old compost.*

2 *The new pot should be a fairly tight fit with about 2.5 cm (1 inch) of space around the tuber. Use fresh potting compost, and put the tuber in the pot so the top is still visible.*

3 *Water it well and put it in a well-lit spot at a temperature of around 16°C (61°F). Water sparingly until the plant is growing strongly and it needs more water.*

SEPTEMBER

THIS IS OFTEN ONE of the most rewarding months of the year, with apples and pears now fruiting abundantly, complemented by autumn-fruiting raspberries and strawberries. There are plenty of autumn flowers around too and the weather now is often better than in the supposedly 'high summer'.

Remember, however, that the colder weather is coming, so harvest and store as much food as you can and, with the borders full to overflowing, now's the time to note which plants will need moving, pruning hard or splitting later.

◀ Annuals can be used for extra summer colour. This border is dominated by the tall, stately flower heads of Nicotiana sylvestris.

GARDENS TO VISIT

- **Barnsley House**, Gloucestershire. Created by gardening writer and designer Rosemary Verey. Beautifully laid out with many attractive plant associations including laburnum arch underplanted with purple ornamental onions (June) and stone path with cushions of rock roses (summer). Lily pond and seventeenth-century summer house. Superb kitchen garden planted for ornamental effect. Plants for sale.
- **Dawyck Botanic Garden**, Scottish Borders. Historic arboretum, part of the Royal Botanic Garden, Edinburgh. Beautiful woodland walks through many rare trees, rhododendrons and shrubs, some trees over three hundred years old. Huge drifts of daffodils in spring. Spectacular autumn colours.
- **Newby Hall**, North Yorkshire. Set around large and elegant house (open). Extensive double herbaceous border. Autumn garden of late-flowering plants, lily pond, rock and water gardens. Woodland and riverside walks. Restaurant, shop and plant centre.
- **Wakehurst Place**, Sussex. The country satellite of the Royal Botanic Gardens, Kew. Collections of rare trees and shrubs in a beautiful setting. Many acid-loving plants. Lakes, water and bog garden.

Looking good

Ornamental grasses are often overlooked in favour of colourful flowers, though they're actually a beautiful and immensely varied group of plants. Several varieties form tall bamboo-like clumps of bold leaves which look particularly good with water, like *Miscanthus sinensis* 'Zebrinus' and 'Gracillimus'. They're tolerant of a range of soils, though some do prefer a moist soil and they can be planted at the edge of the bog garden, including the tufted hair grass (*Deschampsia caespitosa*), Japanese blood grass (*Imperata cylindrica* 'Red Baron') with unusual leaves that are green tipped with dark red, and *Carex* 'Evergold' which forms neat little clumps of evergreen, brightly variegated leaves. In autumn many grasses look exceptionally beautiful when they produce heads of strikingly handsome flower heads. Fountain grass (*Pennisetum*) makes a wonderful display with its purplish flower heads that resemble hairy caterpillars. *Deschampsia* (see above) bears tall clouds of golden flowers, as does *Stipa gigantea*, which looks so striking that it can be grown as a single specimen. Of course, there's the good old pampas grass (*Cortaderia*) which produces masses of feathery plumes. It's an ideal back-of-the-border plant, where its rather dull foliage can be hidden from view, and its flower heads make a sudden and showy appearance in autumn.

Shrubs in flower are less plentiful now than earlier in summer, but there are still some reliable old stalwarts that have been in bloom for weeks, and they'll often continue right up to the frosts. Tree mallow (*Lavatera*) is quick-growing and will provide masses of hollyhock-like flowers for months, even in its first year. Varieties include 'Rosea' (rose-pink), 'Barnsley' (pale pink with a deeper centre), 'Candy Floss' (pale pink) and 'Ice Cool' (white). Hard prune lavateras in early spring.

Potentillas are cheap and cheerful shrubs with lots of bright long-lasting flowers. There are dozens of different varieties in many colours. Yellows are plentiful, like 'Goldfinger', 'Elizabeth', 'Knaphill Seedling' and 'Katherine Dykes'. 'Gold Star' has exceptionally large glowing-yellow flowers. 'Manchu' is one of the best whites, with attractive grey foliage. Brighter colours include 'Red Robin' (orange-red), 'Princess' (pale pink) and 'Tangerine' (copper-orange). Sometimes these brighter flowers can fade in full sun.

Hardy fuchsias are also excellent for stacks of summer flowers. Varieties like 'Alice Hoffman', 'Mrs Popple' and 'Tom Thumb' form small shrubs covered in red and white flowers. 'Genii' is even more attractive with greenish-gold leaves and red flowers.

Lavateras, potentillas and fuchsias are easy to grow, given a reasonable amount of sun.

Full sun is essential for *Hibiscus syriacus*, which needs a little more patience as it often takes several years to begin flowering well. It's well worth the wait, though, as a bush in full flower looks spectacular and exotic. Good varieties include 'Hamabo' (palest pink with a deep red eye), 'Diana' (pure white), 'Blue Bird' (blue with a darker eye) and 'Woodbridge' (deep pink).

Other shrubs in flower include *Abelia*, *Ceratostigma*, *Clerodendrum*, hebes, flowering nutmeg (*Leycesteria formosa*), Russian sage (*Perovskia*), hypericums and tree poppy (*Romneya*).

Climbers flowering now include several that, like hibiscus, need full sun as well as a long hot summer to bloom well. In a good year when they're covered in a glorious display of flowers, you'll forget the lean times when blooms have been few and far between.

Trumpet vine (*Campsis*) is a vigorous scrambling climber which is a breathtaking sight when it produces masses of large, trumpet-shaped, bright orange-red or yellow flowers. Passion flower (*Passiflora*) isn't quite as shy. The easiest one to grow is *P. caerulea* with its curiously shaped blue-and-white flowers. 'Constance Elliott' has beautiful ivory-white ones. There are several other unusual and showy passion flowers, like *P. antioquiensis*, that need conservatory protection in all but the mildest areas. An unusual clematis which needs full sun is *Clematis texensis*, which bears showy tulip-shaped flowers. 'Duchess of Albany' is rose-pink and 'Gravetye Beauty' has ruby-red flowers.

At the easier-to-grow end of the scale, are several other lovely clematis. *Clematis tangutica* and *C. orientalis* bear many little yellow 'lantern' flowers amongst divided sea-green foliage. *C. viticella* varieties are also easy to grow, and they're extremely versatile plants. Because they're quick-growing and benefit from hard annual pruning in spring, they can be grown through large shrubs like lilac or forsythia for added colour, through climbing roses which are also pruned in spring, or even allowed to ramble over ground-cover plants. In the latter case, prune them back in autumn. Of course, they can be grown up walls, fences and pergolas by themselves too. Masses of small colourful flowers are borne for many weeks, often until the first frosts. Varieties include 'Alba Luxurians' (white), 'Etoile Violette' and 'Polish Spirit' (deep purple), 'Madame Julia Correvon' (wine-red) and 'Purpurea Plena Elegans' (rosette-shaped, double purple flowers).

THE GARDEN INDOORS

GROWING BULBS IN POTS

A few pots of spring bulbs can be incredibly cheering, especially when they're flowering indoors in the middle of winter. Hyacinths, narcissi, crocuses, early tulips and dwarf irises can all be forced in pots, to flower well before they would do outside.

The quickest ones to flower are Tazetta narcissi like the strongly scented 'Paper White' and 'Cheerfulness'. Hyacinths are deservedly

Potting hyacinths

popular with their brightly coloured, beautifully scented flowers. For indoor use it's important to buy specially prepared bulbs that have been heat-treated so that they'll flower before spring. To flower at Christmas they'll need to be planted by mid-September.

Plant the bulbs in containers of potting compost or bulb fibre. Ideally the pots should have drainage holes; otherwise you'll need to be very careful not

to over-water as the bulbs could rot. Use bulb fibre for pots without holes as it holds less water than compost. Put a layer of compost in the pot and set the bulbs out on it so that they're not quite touching. Fill the spaces with compost and firm it gently. Larger bulbs like hyacinths should just have their 'noses' exposed, while smaller ones should be just covered. Water the pots and put them in a cool dark place, either outdoors in a box or frame, or in a shed. They need to be completely dark and cold to encourage roots and leaves to form, so the pots should be covered with black polythene or buried under a thick layer of sand or bark.

Check them regularly to make sure that the compost is still moist, and water sparingly if necessary. Move into the light once the shoots are 2.5–5 cm (1–2 in) high (see page 181).

September

PLANT OF THE MONTH

Cape figwort *(Phygelius).*
HEIGHT: 60 cm–1.8 m (2 6 ft)
SPREAD: 45 cm–1m (1½–3 ft)
FLOWERING TIME: August–October
POSITION: Sun
SOIL: Well-drained **HARDY?**: Yes

The Cape figwort is a handsome and unusual plant for
late summer colour, and it's surprisingly easy to grow. It
produces tall flower spikes clothed with many drooping
tubular flowers in a range of attractive and unusual colours,
including 'Yellow Trumpet' (creamy-yellow), 'Devil's Tears'
(deep reddish-pink with orange-red edges) and 'African
Queen' (pale red).

This plant can be grown in two ways. It can be treated as
a shrub and trained against a sunny wall, where it can reach
around 1.8 m (6 ft). Alternatively, grow it in a border like a
herbaceous perennial, cutting it back in spring almost to
ground level. In the coldest areas it's best planted near a
sheltered wall.

142

◄ *Bright colours dominate the border as autumn approaches. Tall orange-red 'pokers' of kniphofia and glowing red penstemons tone with the large, dark purple leaves of heuchera.*

General tasks

Autumn planting is traditional and best for all hardy garden plants. Hardier evergreens like rhododendrons can be planted now, but those evergreens that could suffer from frost damage are best planted in spring (see page 86).

Conditions in autumn are ideal to help plants establish quickly. The soil is warm and the weather is rarely dry for long periods. Plant growth is slowing down in readiness for winter, which means that plants are not under stress from trying to make leaf and root growth at the same time, as they would be in spring or summer. In all but the coldest weather through the winter, they'll be making lots of roots and they'll be well established in readiness to explode into growth in spring.

Prepare the ground thoroughly before planting. Dig the ground over two spades deep, pull out all weeds and especially the roots of perennial ones, and incorporate plenty of well-rotted manure or garden compost. At least an hour before planting, water the plant well. Dig a hole large enough to take the plant's rootball and mix a handful of organic fertilizer into the hole and the excavated soil.

Take off the pot carefully (polythene ones can be cut off) and put the plant in the hole so that the top of the rootball is at soil level. Backfill with soil and firm it thoroughly with your heel, then water the plant well. Stake trees and tie them securely with a plastic tree tie.

In exposed sites, newly planted conifers and evergreens can be killed by freezing winter winds. Surround them with a windbreak of polythene or fine netting until spring.

If you're buying roses, fruit trees or bushes, and hedging plants, wait until October or November when the new crop of bare-rooted or root-wrapped plants is available. You'll get really healthy, fresh plants and they're usually cheaper than container-grown ones too.

Clay soil that hasn't been cultivated before is best dug over in autumn while it's dry and reasonably manageable. Roughly dig the ground and leave the soil in large lumps over winter so that the frost can help break it down. A green manure crop can also help improve the soil (see below).

Green manure plants can be sown on any ground that will be left bare until spring. They'll take up nutrients, therefore preventing them being washed out of the soil during winter. In spring they'll be dug into the ground to rot down, improving the soil structure and releasing nutrients. Winter tares, winter field beans and grazing rye can be sown now. Grazing rye is particularly useful for heavy ground as its extensive roots help break up the soil.

Moving established shrubs is best done in autumn, for the same reasons as autumn planting (see above). There's always a risk that plants will die, especially long-established ones, but their chances can be improved by careful preparation, handling, and aftercare.

CREATE A FLOWERING PILLAR

If your garden's a bit flat, make a leafy flowering column several feet high by simply banging in a stout 2.4-m (8-ft) post towards the middle of the border. Plant a rambler rose on one side and a late-flowering clematis on the other. *C. viticella* varieties are ideal. Right from the start you should train the rose tightly round the post to keep it neat and encourage flowering. After flowering, cut out the older shoots and train in new ones.

The clematis will find its own way through the rose to flower in late summer, after which, the old stems are cut off at ground level and pulled out of the rose to give it light and air. The clematis will happily regrow the following year and both plants will get better and better every season.

If you know several months in advance that plants have to be shifted, dig a deep narrow trench in a circle about 60 cm– 1 m (2–3 ft) from the plant's stem, and then refill it. This severs long roots and encourages the plant to produce a compact rootball.

Moving a large shrub is usually a two-person job. Prepare the new planting hole first. Tie in the plant's branches to give yourself some space and to minimize damage. Then dig a narrow trench completely round the shrub, keeping as much soil round the roots as possible. Once the roots are all severed, work a sheet of hessian or strong polythene right underneath the plant and tie it around the stem so that the whole rootball is wrapped securely. The easiest way to transport a large plant is to tie a strong stake to its stem just above ground level, so that it can be easily carried by two people. Put the plant in its new hole and remove the hessian or polythene. Backfill with soil and firm it thoroughly.

It's important to give the plant a good soaking at once, and to keep it well watered through next spring and summer. To make sure that the whole rootball gets water, take a couple of short lengths of large rigid pipe (like drainpipe) and pierce holes in them. Put them either side of the rootball before backfilling with soil. They can be filled at each watering to soak the roots thoroughly.

▲ *When moving a large shrub wrap sacking or polythene securely round the rootball to keep as much soil as possible attached to it.*

▶ *Tie a stout stake to the stem of the shrub so that two people can lift it.*

Ornamental garden

▶ Sedum spectabile *looks marvellous in autumn with its flat heads of pink flowers. Both this plant and the blue catmint in the foreground are popular with butterflies.*

ANNUALS AND BIENNIALS

Biennials for spring flowering, like wallflowers and polyanthus, can be planted out if summer-flowering annuals have finished. Revitalize the ground first by digging in some garden compost and organic fertilizer. Pinch out the tips of the plants to encourage bushy growth, and water them well during dry spells.

Hardy annuals can be sown outside where they're to flower next year, provided the soil is well-drained. They'll look most natural growing in irregular patches, but sow them in several straight shallow drills about 15 cm (6 in) apart within each area. This makes weeding easier when the seeds have germinated. See pages 36 and 53 for varieties.

Grasses can be used to make an effective contrast with flowering plants. The blue agapanthus at the back of the border should be planted in the spring, but the pampas grass is best put in this month or next.

On heavy soil where there's a danger of the seeds rotting over winter, sow them in modules under cover for planting out in spring (see page 153). Alternatively, sow direct in spring. Sow sweet peas in autumn for sturdy early-flowering plants. Direct sowing gives the best plants so long as the soil isn't too heavy, though it's safer to hedge your bets in case of a severe winter and sow some in pots under cover as well.

BULBS

Spring bulbs can all be planted this month, except tulips. These are best planted in October or even November, as they're more susceptible to disease than other bulbs and early planting increases the risk of attack. Daffodils and narcissi should be planted by the end of the month as they need plenty of time to make root growth. See page 132 for planting details.

Containers can be planted up with bulbs for a glorious spring display. There's no need to renew the compost completely after the summer-flowering annuals have been pulled out – just revitalize it with some fresh garden compost and a handful of bone meal. Alternatively, use the compost from old growing bags. Pack the bulbs in to make a really stunning show. Either plant just one variety per pot, or put several differ-ent ones together in layers for a succession of colour. For example, daffodils at the bottom, dwarf tulips in the middle and crocuses on top, finishing off with a few winter-flowering pansies. You'll have colour from winter until well into spring.

Drainage is essential for bulbs as waterlogged ones will rot. The pots must have drainage holes in the bottom, covered by a layer of broken clay pots or gravel. It helps to raise them a little way off the ground using special pot feet, bits of wood or pieces of old paving slabs. Stand the pots in a sheltered spot, preferably against a house wall, to protect them from severe frosts.

LAWN

An established lawn needs feeding now, but only if it wasn't given a spring and summer feed. Fertilizer applied now should be low in nitrogen.

If you're aiming for a perfect lawn, rake the grass to remove the 'thatch' (a layer of dead grass) and moss. Aerate the lawn if there have been problems with drainage (see page 15).

Autumn is also a good time to carry out any renovations, like seeding bare patches, repairing edges or levelling out bumps and hollows. Top dressing the whole lawn will improve its condition enormously (see page 162).

TIPS FOR CHOOSING TURF

- The two main sorts are meadow and cultivated turf. Meadow turf is cut from managed pasture land. It's cheapest and makes a reasonable hard-wearing lawn, but quality can vary considerably. Cultivated turf is specially grown with a variety of seed mixtures, so it's better quality and you can choose from different types of grasses, but it's about two and a half times more expensive. Nevertheless, the quality is always superb and it's highly recommended.

- Compare prices from local garden centres and turf suppliers. Don't forget to take delivery charges and VAT into account. Try to see samples beforehand if you're ordering a lot of turf.
- Inspect the turves on delivery. Reject any that are dry, yellowing, contain lots of weeds, or that fall apart easily. Cultivated turves should be completely weed-free.
- Specify a convenient delivery date when you can lay the turf immediately.

TURFING A NEW LAWN

Turfing can be done at any time of year unless the ground is frozen. Autumn is ideal, however, because the ground is warm and there's normally enough rain to help the grass establish quickly and to make watering unnecessary.

To lay turf, first prepare the ground well in advance (see page 25). Make sure that the preparation will be completed before the turf is delivered, as it shouldn't be left rolled up for more than a couple of days. If laying the lawn is unavoidably delayed, unroll the turves to expose the grass to the light and don't let them dry out.

After all the turf has been laid, keep it well watered using a sprinkler and moving it round regularly to apply the water little and often. If you allow it to dry out, it'll shrink to leave ugly spaces. In spring or summer it's essential to water the lawn during dry weather for a couple of months, but at this time of year it's rarely necessary.

Autumn is also a good time to sow new lawns (see page 40).

1 *Lay the edging turves in a strip around the lawn, unrolling the turf slowly and carefully.*

2 *Tap the turf firmly with the back of a rake so it makes good contact with the soil.*

3 *At the end of each row, lay the last turf over the edging turf and cut off the excess with an old knife.*

4 *Continue to lay the turf in rows, pulling each one firmly in with the back of the rake.*

There's lots of late summer colour in the herbaceous border, including yellow golden rod and rudbeckias. Make a note to divide any overcrowded clumps in autumn or late winter.

Kitchen garden

FRUIT

Apples and pears should be harvested when the fruit separates easily from the branch. To store apples, select undamaged fruits and put about 1 kg (2 lb) at a time into sealed polythene bags, pierced with a couple of pin-holes. Store pears in open wooden trays or on shelves. Keep both fruits in a very cool but just frost-free place. Check the fruits regularly and throw out any with signs of rot.

If you've got masses of fruit, even windfalls, it's worth storing some in boxes to put out for the birds in winter. Blackbirds, thrushes, redwings and field-fares will really appreciate such a feast when the weather's cold.

Grease bands fixed round the trunks of apple trees will trap the wingless female winter moths as they climb up the trunk to lay their eggs. The caterpillars would otherwise feed on the opening buds and young leaves.

Strawberries should be planted by the end of September so that they can establish well for cropping next year. Prepare the ground thoroughly by digging in well-rotted compost or manure, and rake in some organic fertilizer. Space the plants 45 x 60 cm (1½ x 2 ft) apart, with the crown of the plant exactly at soil level. Water well after planting.

VEGETABLES

Asparagus foliage should be cut down to within 2.5 cm (1 in) of the ground once it has turned yellow, and the plants should then be mulched with well-rotted manure. Prepare a site for asparagus crowns to be planted next spring by digging in manure.

Marrows, pumpkins and squashes can be picked and put in the sun to ripen for a few days. Then hang them in net bags in a dry frost-free place, and they'll keep for two or three months.

◄ *Fixing grease-bands round apple trees in autumn will help control winter moth.*

▼ *Squashes can be stored if they're picked when mature and ripened in the sun.*

151

Garlic should be planted in autumn and preferably before December, as it needs a cold period to grow successfully.

Although you can plant garlic bought from the greengrocer, it's advisable to buy specially cultivated bulbs because they are of better quality.

Garlic needs a sunny site, preferably on well-drained soil. On heavy ground, plant it on ridges of soil. Break each bulb into separate cloves, and plant each one 7.5–10 cm (3–4 in) apart with 30 cm (1 ft) between rows. The tops of the cloves should be just below the surface of the ground. If there's any danger of water-logging or if the ground isn't ready, plant in modules for spring planting. Stand the trays in a sheltered spot outside.

Root vegetables like beetroot, carrots, parsnips and turnips can be lifted and stored for winter use. Parsnips, Hamburg parsley and swedes are best left in the ground to be frosted since this improves the flavour, though they're liable to be attacked by pests. To store other root crops, select undamaged roots and twist or cut the leaves off first, leaving a few centimetres of stem. (Wear gloves for doing beetroot if you don't want purple hands!) Put the roots in a wooden box, separated with dry sand, and store them in a cool but frost-free place. Inspect them regularly and throw out any with signs of rot.

Potatoes should be lifted on a sunny day and spread out on the ground for an hour or two until they're dry. Store undamaged ones in paper sacks, again in a frost-free place. Remember to check them from time to time in case any have started to rot.

Lettuce can be sown outside in rows and covered with cloches next month for a winter crop, or sown in the greenhouse or coldframe. Choose a variety specially bred for autumn sowing like 'Fivia' or 'Novita'.

Spring cabbage can be planted 15 cm (6 in) apart in rows 30 cm (1ft) apart so that every other plant can be harvested for spring greens, leaving the rest to heart up.

Freshly dug potatoes are a real delight and packed full of flavour. For storing, lift potatoes on a dry, sunny day.

Greenhouse and windowsill

Bulbs can be planted in pots to brighten up the greenhouse. Dwarf varieties are ideal as their small flowers can be fully appreciated at close quarters, and they shouldn't need staking. There are lots of good varieties, like the dwarf *Narcissus canaliculatus* with yellow and white scented flowers, 'Jack Snipe' with creamy-yellow swept-back petals, and 'Minimus' with yellow flowers on tiny stems. Dwarf tulip species, glory of the snow (*Chionodoxa*), crocus and dwarf iris are all well worth growing.

Growing bags can be used again after tomatoes and other crops have been harvested. Sow or plant out fast-maturing salad crops like lettuce, mustard and cress, or radish, but make sure that you liquid-feed them.

Hardy annuals make excellent and inexpensive flowering pot plants. Sown now in the unheated greenhouse or cold-frame, they'll provide masses of colour next spring and early summer. Simply sow a pinch of seed in 10–13-cm (4–5-in) pots and thin the seedlings to leave three or four strong ones. Choose compact varieties for pot plants, like pot marigold (*Calendula* 'Baby Orange'), cornflower 'Florence', *Godetia* 'Azaleaflora', *Clarkia* 'Snowflake' and stock 'Cinderella'.

Hardy annuals can also be sown in modules for planting out next spring. Sow a small pinch of seed in each module and leave the seedlings unthinned.

Prepare the greenhouse for winter towards the end of the month. If your greenhouse is full of tomatoes, cucumbers or other vegetables, wait until they've finished cropping.

Choose a fine still day so that plants can be safely stood outside. Remove shading, clean out gutters and downpipes, and wash the glass inside and out. Wooden-framed greenhouses may need treating with a timber preservative. Take out, clean and dry capillary matting, then put it away for the winter. Wash the staging with hot water and disinfectant. Remove any debris and weeds on the floor and underneath the staging, which can shelter pests and diseases. While the greenhouse is empty, it's well worth insulating it by fixing bubble polythene inside the walls and roof. Set up the heater, and you'll be ready to keep your plants snug in case of early frosts.

Unheated greenhouses needn't be lacking in colour over winter. Lots of flowering plants will grow happily without heat so long as they're protected from the worst ravages of the winter weather.

As well as bulbs and hardy annuals (see above), many hardy winter and early spring-flowering garden plants can be grown in tubs where they'll flourish under cover. *Daphne*, *Pieris* and Christmas box (*Sarcococca*) will fill the greenhouse with scent and colour, while others like camellias and Christmas rose (*Helleborus niger*) will produce masses of beautiful flowers. There are also lots of shrubs on the border of hardiness that can be grown in tubs to spend winter under cover (see page 86).

CHECKLIST

- Reduce watering and ventilation in the greenhouse as the temperature drops.
- Continue taking cuttings of tender perennials.
- Ornamental onions (*Allium*) are best planted in autumn.
- Finish lifting and storing onions and garlic.
- Stake mature Brussels sprout plants.
- Lift, divide and replant early spring-flowering perennials.
- Bring in pot plants that were put out for the summer.

OCTOBER

GARDENERS NEED to be on their toes now. It may seem an odd thing to advise in this book, but remember that you simply can't garden by the calendar. In the south or, indeed, even on the Gulf Stream-warmed west coast of Scotland, you'll not be worrying about the hardest frosts until at least next month. In the north-east you could be clobbered well before then. If you live in a harsher area, it's best to get tender plants protected now, and even in milder climes you need to keep a weather eye on the forecast.

On the brighter side, however, this is the best month of all for glowing red, orange and yellow autumn foliage colour and wonderful for fruits and berries too.

◀ *The tall, creamy-white plumes of pampas grass (*Cortaderia selloana*) make a stunning centrepiece to this border, and they're further emphasised by a dark-foliaged conifer in the background.*

GARDENS TO VISIT

- **Felbrigg Hall**, Norfolk. Famous for its collection of *Colchicum*. Other features include an orangery, a dovecote, vine house, a restored walled garden and woodland walks.
- **Logan Botanic Garden**, Dumfries and Galloway. Part of the Royal Botanic Garden, Edinburgh. Mild westerly location means many exotic southern-hemisphere plants can be grown in large walled garden, including tree ferns and cabbage palms (*Cordyline*). Shop and restaurant.
- **Muncaster Castle**, Cumbria. Large collection of rhododendrons, camellias and azaleas look magnificent in spring/early summer. Many attractive shrubs and trees, good autumn colour. Garden centre, shop and café.
- **Westonbirt Arboretum**, Gloucestershire. Famous for spectacular autumn colours. Many flowering shrubs including eucryphias in summer, evergreens and colourful bark in winter. Shop and restaurant.

Looking good

Autumn leaves make a wonderful pageant of colour from now until they finally fall. Not all garden plants have good autumn leaf colour, though, so it's something worth bearing in mind when choosing plants. The flaming reds, oranges and yellows of autumn foliage are among the great joys of the gardening year.

All the Japanese maples (*Acer palmatum* varieties) have superb autumn colour and a great range of foliage shapes too. Top varieties are 'Atropurpureum' (purple leaves turning bright red), 'Osakazuki' (green turning bright crimson) and 'Seiryu' (green turning orange-yellow and crimson). The large, lobed leaves of the oak-leaved hydrangea (*Hydrangea quercifolia*) are brightly tinted with shades of red, and this is one hydrangea that prefers a sunny spot. The shrubby plumbago (*Ceratostigma*) is a late-flowering dwarf shrub with pretty, deep blue flowers that make a beautiful contrast to the bright red of its autumn leaves. Climbers like *Vitis coignetiae* with its enormous lobed leaves turning deep bronze-red in autumn, and Virginia creeper (*Parthenocissus quinquefolia*), take up lots of wall space, but a large expanse covered with fiery red autumn foliage is a truly breathtaking sight. *P. henryana* is the best variety for spring and summer interest because its lobed leaves are attractively veined with white.

Acid-loving shrubs develop the most intense colours of all. *Fothergilla* turns rich shades of yellow and orange, so that the bush appears to be on fire. Deciduous azaleas colour beautifully, as does *Enkianthus campanulatus* which bears many delicate pink, urn-shaped flowers in spring. Snowy mespilus (*Amelanchier lamarckii*) colours much more deeply on acid soil, turning red if it's in the sun and yellow in shade.

You may have to search out some of the less usual trees, but they're well worth the extra effort because they really stand out from the crowd in autumn. *Cercidiphyllum japonicum* has attractive rounded leaves that turn shades of yellow and pink. After the first frosts, they smell deliciously of burnt sugar and a bit like candy-floss. *Stuartia pseudocamellia* slowly grows to form a small tree with attractive flaking bark and leaves that turn red and yellow. *Nyssa sinensis* forms a small spreading tree with leaves turning all shades of red. These last two need a lime-free soil, so make sure that you test yours before buying either of them.

Berries are an invaluable source of food for birds. They prefer red and orange, so the white, yellow or pink ones will be left until last or not even touched in a mild winter. It's worth planting a mixture – some for you to enjoy and some for the birds.

Rowans (*Sorbus*) are excellent year-round trees with flowers in spring, masses of berries in autumn, and attractively shaped foliage too. Mountain ash or rowan (*Sorbus aucuparia*) is a particular bird favourite and it's usually weighed down with bunches of red fruits. Good garden varieties include 'Sheerwater Seedling' and 'Cardinal Royal' which form upright heads of branches. 'Aspleniifolia' has fern-like foliage, while 'Embley' has glowing red autumn leaves too. For longer-lasting fruits, *S. hupehensis* 'Pink Pagoda' bears pinkish-white berries, *S. cashmiriana* has gleaming white ones and 'Golden Wonder' bears glowing yellow fruits.

Crab apples (*Malus*) are, like rowans, good all-year trees, with attractive spring flowers and autumn fruits. Birds and even butterflies feed on the fallen fruit, and if you can get there first it can be used to make delicious crab apple jelly. 'John Downie' is the best culinary variety with its large orange-and-red fruits, but for ornament choose one which holds its fruit for a long time, like

'Golden Hornet' with deep yellow fruits or 'Red Sentinel' which has dark red ones. Bear in mind that they'll also pollinate apple trees.

Many berry-bearing shrubs tend to be on the large side and not suited to tiny gardens. Spindle bush (*Euonymus europaeus*) is covered with red fruits that split open into quarters to reveal orange seeds. 'Red Cascade' is the best variety with good autumn leaf colour too. The guelder rose (*Viburnum opulus*) has white flowers in early summer followed by heavy clusters of red berries. Those of 'Fructuluteo' and 'Xanthocarpum' are yellow, while the red-berried 'Compactum' reaches only 1 m (3 ft). Sea buckthorn (*Hippophae rhamnoides*) has attractive, narrow, silvery leaves and bears bright orange-yellow berries. It's an excellent seaside shrub because it tolerates salt-laden winds.

Herbaceous perennials provide much of the flower colour in the autumn garden. Those in warm glowing shades are particularly welcome as the weather becomes colder.

Michaelmas daisies (*Aster*) include many bright reds and pinks, but most are martyrs to mildew, a disfiguring fungal disease. So look out for the mildew-free *Aster* x *frikartii* 'Mönch', which bears tall stems of clear lavender-blue flowers that appear in late summer and last for months. *A. thomsonii* 'Nanus' is like a miniature version, growing to around 30 cm (1 ft), and flowers for just as long.

Asters look great planted with Japanese anemones, which also flower for a long time and bear beautiful pink or white flowers on tall stems. They can become invasive, but they're easy to control with a spade and it's well worth it because their flowers are nothing short of superb, and they're good for cutting.

Sedum spectabile is an invaluable autumn perennial with its large flat heads of dark pink flowers. Divide it and replant every year though, or it tends to flop. 'Brilliant' has vivid pink flowers and 'Autumn Joy' is rich deep pink. They look particularly good with blue flowers, like the poisonous monkshoods (*Aconitum*), such as *A. napellus*, with their tall spikes of hooded flowers. Monkshoods are happy in shade, as is bear's breeches (*Acanthus*) which has tall handsome spikes of mauve-and-white flowers above clumps of large glossy leaves, and toad lily (*Tricyrtis*) which has unusual mauve-and-white spotted flowers borne on tall stems.

Autumn-flowering bulbs like autumn crocus (*Colchicum*) are lovely for naturalizing under trees or just planted in borders among other plants. In spring they produce big tufts of green leaves which die back by summer, then in autumn their pink-and-white flowers appear almost magically from bare ground – hence another of their names, 'naked ladies'. *Cyclamen hederifolium* are delightful little plants with purple flowers and marbled leaves. They're particularly good for growing underneath mature trees and hedges where little else will survive.

IMPROVING YOUR SOIL

The soil is the gardener's raw material and needs to be respected, nurtured and loved – and that means plenty of bulky organic matter of one kind or another. Ideally it should be dug in every year on at least part of the plot, though for many gardeners that's easier said than done. Manure's scarce and the alternatives are expensive; however, if you take action now, there is an answer.

You may well have to collect it, but straw is cheap and plentiful. So cheap, in fact, that it could be worth your while getting together with friends and hiring a trailer to collect a load of bales. Used right now, they'll do the job a treat. It has always been considered by gardeners and agricultural scientists alike that digging in straw on its own would rob the soil of nitrogen. The bacteria that rot it down use nitrogen as a fuel. If you don't supply it, they take it from the soil. But it's been found that, provided you dig it in early, there's no loss. Certainly the bacteria remove nitrogen in the first instance but, by the time you come to sow in the spring, they've done their job, died off and returned it to the soil.

The moral, of course, is to get digging just as soon as you can.

PLANT OF THE MONTH

Kaffir lily *(Schizostylis)*
HEIGHT: 60 cm (2 ft)
SPREAD: 60 cm (2 ft)
FLOWERING TIME: September–November
POSITION: Sun
SOIL: Any except light, dry soils
HARDY?: Yes

The Kaffir lily is the latest of all perennials to flower. Although it starts producing its stems of pretty cupped flowers early in autumn, if the weather permits it'll even flower until December. Alternatively, grow it in a tub and bring it under cover to prolong flowering. It needs plenty of moisture in summer to flower well and a sunny spot, so dig in lots of compost or manure before planting.

The flowers are shades of red, pink and white: 'Major' has attractive crimson flowers, 'Cardinal', dark red ones, 'Mrs Hegarty' is a lovely soft pink, 'Sunrise' is bright pink and 'Alba' is pure white. The Kaffir lily is a vigorous plant, quickly forming a clump of neat grassy foliage, which is best divided every three or four years to encourage lots of flowers.

◀ *In early autumn
the borders are still
chock-full of flowers.
Perennials like
Michaelmas daisies,
phlox, golden rod
and rudbeckias are
blazing with colour*

General tasks

Bare-rooted plants like trees, shrubs, roses and fruit bushes will be available from the middle of the month onwards. Plants supplied by mail order are often bare-rooted.

Prepare the ground in advance by digging it over and mixing in lots of compost or well-rotted manure. Add some more compost to the planting hole. Unpack plants as soon as they arrive, and give their roots a good soak in a bucket for a couple of hours if they look at all dry. Then cover the roots so that they don't dry out and keep them protected from frost. If planting is delayed for more than a few days, heel them in by digging a trench and covering the roots with soil.

Plant roses and black currants a few centimetres deeper than they were growing previously, to encourage shoots to grow directly from the ground. Plant all others at the same depth as before. Trees need staking with a stout wooden stake that comes about a third of the way up the stem. With bare-rooted plants, it's best to put it in before you plant the tree to avoid damaging the roots.

Berries can be collected from shrubs and trees and sown straight away. Squeeze the seeds out of their surrounding pulp and sow them in a compost of equal parts soil, coarse grit and coir compost. Put the pots in a coldframe.

Fallen leaves should be raked up within a few days where they're covering lawns and plants, or they could yellow and damage foliage. Leaves can be left to rot down on bare soil. Make leafmould by storing collected leaves in a wire-netting container, or in black polythene bags with a few holes pierced in the sides. In a year or so you'll have a wonderful soil conditioner.

Tall deciduous shrubs like roses, tree mallow (*Lavatera*) and butterfly bush (*Buddleia*) that will be pruned in early spring are best cut back by about a third now to prevent wind-rocking.

Tubs cleared of summer-flowering plants can be planted with biennials and bulbs for a gorgeous display of spring colour. Ornamental cabbages are also good plants for winter colour, with attractively shaped heads of white, green or purple foliage. They're not cheap to buy, though they're fairly easy to grow from seed (see page 93).

There are also lots of colourful evergreens suitable for containers that will really cheer up your patio for the winter. Good ones include *Euonymus japonicus* varieties like 'Marieke' and 'Aureopictus' with green-and-gold leaves. Variegated box (*Buxus*) like 'Elegantissima', 'Gold Tip' and 'Aurea Marginata' can be clipped into attractive balls or pyramids. Dwarf conifers are available in loads of shapes and colours, and they really come into their own in winter when they give the garden some much-needed structure.

A simple wire netting container is all that's needed to make leafmould, which is a wonderful soil conditioner.

Ornamental garden

ANNUALS, BIENNIALS AND TENDER PERENNIALS

Spring bedding plants like wallflowers and forget-me-nots are best planted in their flowering positions by the end of the month on heavy soil, though there's a bit more leeway with light soils. It may mean lifting summer-flowering annuals while they're still flowering, but smaller plants like busy Lizzies (*Impatiens*) and *Begonia semperflorens* can be potted up and put on a well-lit windowsill or in the greenhouse. They should continue flowering for weeks, if not months.

Chrysanthemums, except for a few hardy varieties, must be lifted and stored, as for dahlias (see below). Cut them back to 10 cm (4 in) before lifting.

Tender perennials should be lifted before the first frosts, potted and kept in a frost-free place for the winter. Some will make well-established plants to put out next spring, but others, like geraniums and marguerites, are much better grown again from cuttings for next season. The plants you lift and store will provide plenty of cuttings in the spring.

Lift the plants carefully and cut back any tall leggy shoots. Trim off dead flowers and any damaged growth, and pull away dead leaves. Gently shake off surplus soil and pot the plant into a snug-fitting pot, using a coir compost. If space is limited, pack them closely together in boxes and cover the roots with compost.

African daisies (*Osteospermum*, *Gazania* and *Arctotis*), *Lantana*, *Argyranthemum* and other tender perennials can be kept indoors or in a frost-free greenhouse. Keep the soil just moist over winter. Fuchsias should be potted but the soil should be kept virtually dry, and they're best stored on their sides under the greenhouse staging.

Plants with tuberous roots like marvel of Peru (*Mirabilis jalapa*) and chocolate plant (*Cosmos atrosanguineus*) should be stored as for dahlias (see below).

Geraniums, *Felicia* and busy Lizzies (*Impatiens*) make excellent houseplants as they continue to produce lots of flowers. Petunias can be potted up and cut back, and they too will soon produce new shoots and flowers.

If you haven't got a heated place in which to store your tender perennials, it's worth trying to keep them in an unheated greenhouse or coldframe that's well insulated with bubble polythene, but of course there's always a risk of losing plants in severely cold spells. It's vital not to over-water, but to keep the compost just slightly moist.

BULBS

Tender bulbs and tubers like gladioli, dahlias, climbing nasturtium (*Tropaeolum tuberosum*), chocolate plant (*Cosmos atrosanguineus*) and marvel of Peru (*Mirabilis jalapa*) should be lifted before the first hard frost and stored for the winter. Lift gladioli, shake off the soil and cut off the stems, leaving a short piece attached to each corm. Spread them out in an airy frost-free spot to dry for a couple of weeks. When they're completely dry, clean them by breaking off the old, shrivelled corm at the base and rubbing off the dry outer skin. Store them in paper bags in a dry, cool, frost-free place.

The little cormlets can be stored separately and planted in pots next spring, though they'll take at least three years to reach flowering size.

You have to be a bit careful with plants like dahlias because it's easy to spear them with a fork. Cut back the foliage to within a few centimetres of the tuber. Then stand them upside-down for a day so that the moisture drains out of their hollow stems. Put the tubers upright into wooden boxes and cover with soil or old compost, leaving their crowns just visible. Store them in a cool frost-free place and keep the soil very slightly moist.

HERBACEOUS PERENNIALS

Cut back the dead foliage of all perennials, any time from now until spring. If you can put up with your borders looking a bit scruffy, delay tidying up until early spring. The dead foliage provides winter shelter for ladybirds and other beneficial insects like ground beetles, a bit of food for birds and, when it's covered with hoar frost it looks wonderful.

Clean up pampas grass (*Cortaderia*), cutting off or pulling out dead leaves. But don't ever do it without wearing strong gloves as the leaves have sharp edges. One popular method is to burn off the dead foliage, but this isn't a good idea. Not only can it damage the plant, but you'll also kill lots of useful hibernating insects.

Perennials can be lifted and divided when they've formed large clumps, usually after three or four years (see page 37). Late-flowering varieties like Michaelmas daisy (*Aster*) and red hot poker (*Kniphofia*) are best left until spring.

LAWN

An established lawn should be mown less frequently as growth slows down; mowing can usually stop around the end of the month.

Rake out the 'thatch' (a layer of dead grass) if you wish, and aerate the lawn if drainage is poor (see pages 15 and 25).

Top-dressing can improve all types of lawn by revitalizing the upper layer of soil and increasing the rooting area. First rake out the thatch and mow the grass. Mix up a compost of three parts of sieved garden soil, two parts of sharp sand and one part of sieved compost (coconut-fibre if you wish). Spread a 1–2-cm (½–1-in) layer over the lawn and work it in well with the back of a rake, but take care not to smother the grass completely. It'll look messy for a couple of weeks but the grass soon grows through. If the lawn is rather sparse or worn, mix a bit of grass seed in with the compost.

A new lawn can still be seeded or turfed. Ideally finish seeding by the end of the month. Water a lawn laid last month if the weather's dry.

SHRUBS

Hardwood cuttings can be taken from deciduous shrubs any time over winter. Now is the best time, however, when the plants have just lost their leaves and the soil still has some warmth to help speed rooting.

Take cuttings around 20–25 cm (8–10 in) long from straight healthy shoots, making a straight cut on the base

---

SOWING HARDY ANNUALS

Hardy annuals can be sown outside where they are to flower, so long as the soil is well-drained. Otherwise, delay sowing until spring.

1 *Annuals look best when they're growing in irregularly-shaped patches, and these are easily marked out with sand. Then use a bamboo cane to make shallow drills for the seeds within each patch.*

2 *Sow the seeds thinly in the drills and cover them with a little soil. Sowing them in several short rows means it's easy to distinguish between the germinating seeds and weeds.*

THE GARDEN INDOORS

HERBS FOR WINTER

Herbs growing outside will mostly die back over winter, but with a bit of forward planning you can keep using your own herbs right through the coldest months.

You can't beat fresh-picked herbs for flavour. Favourites like mint, sage and parsley can be potted up in late summer and brought inside this month to provide you with fresh foliage all winter (see page 136). Parsley growing outside can also be covered with cloches.

Dried herbs can be kept near to hand in the kitchen. Cut the fresh foliage early on a fine day, tie the sprigs in small bunches and hang them upside-down to dry in a cool airy room – not the bathroom or kitchen. Alternatively spread the foliage out on baking trays and put them in a very low oven with the door open. Once the leaves are dry and crisp to the touch, gently pull the leaves off the stems and store them in clean dry jars.

Yet another way to preserve herbs is to wash the leaves, chop them up and put them in ice-cube trays. Cover with a little water and freeze them.

Many dried herbs can be used to make refreshing herb teas, like peppermint, chamomile, lemon balm, lemon verbena and sage. Simply put a good teaspoon of the dried herb in a cup, pour on boiling water and leave to stand for five minutes before removing the leaves. Some people prefer herb teas sweetened with a little honey.

just below a leaf joint. Trim off the soft top growth. Dip the base in hormone rooting liquid or powder.

Make a slit trench, in either the cold-frame or outside, by pushing the spade into the ground and rocking it backwards and forwards. If the trench is outside, put about 5 cm (2 in) of sharp sand in the base to encourage rooting. Put the cuttings in, spaced 10–15 cm (4–6 in) apart, and with about 7.5 cm (3 in) of stem above ground. Firm the soil around them.

Check the cuttings during winter and refirm them if they've been lifted by frost. Rooting normally takes a year.

WATER GARDEN

Fish should be given less food as the weather becomes colder and their activity level drops.

Floating plants like water hyacinth will be killed by frost. Take out a few young plantlets and put them in a large jar half-filled with water and with a little soil in the bottom. Keep it on a cool windowsill.

Ponds should be tidied up in preparation for winter. Cut back dead marginal plants to just above water level. Take out any dead leaves and blanketweed, and trim back oxygenating plants that have made lots of growth. Fix a net over the pond to prevent fallen leaves blowing in, as they'll sink to the bottom and rot.

Submersible pumps should be taken out and stored over winter. Clean the pump and its filter in fresh water, leave it to dry and store it in a frost-free place. Drain and insulate surface pumps.

Kitchen garden

FRUIT

Peaches and nectarines that were sprayed with copper fungicide earlier in the year, to protect them from peach leaf curl, should be sprayed again around the time the leaves fall.

Berry fruits like blackberries, loganberries and tayberries should be pruned after harvest. Cut out all the old stems which have borne fruit and tie the new ones in their place. If all the stems have been allowed to grow together, pruning is something of a battle, so it's much easier to keep them separate by training the new stems to one side only. The shoots produced next spring can then be trained to the other side.

Black currants should now be pruned. Cut back newly planted bushes to about 7.5 cm (3 in) from the ground (**1**). On mature bushes, remove about a third to a half of the oldest branches (**2**). Raspberries that are newly planted should be cut back to 15 cm (6 in). The resulting canes produced this season should have their soft tips removed (**1**). This hard pruning encourages the growth of many new shoots next spring (**2**).

VEGETABLES

Root vegetables like leeks can be left in the ground and lifted as they're required through the winter. Cover the surrounding soil with a layer of straw to prevent it becoming too frozen to allow lifting.

Continue lifting and storing other root vegetables (see 152). Salsify and scorzonera can also be stored in the same way.

Seakale can be forced, either indoors or outside *in situ*, from now until January. The blanched stems make an unusual winter vegetable.

Plants growing outside can be forced for several years in succession. Cut off the yellowing leaves and clear any debris. Put a 10-cm (4-in) layer of straw on top of the crowns for insulation, then place a large lightproof bucket or pot upside-down over the plant. The stems will be ready in about three months.

Indoor forcing is quicker, but the plants can be used only once. Put several crowns in a large pot of good garden soil or compost, with the tops just below soil level. Set an upturned pot on top so that they're in complete darkness. Keep the soil just moist and the temperature at around 16°C (60°F).

Pruning black currants

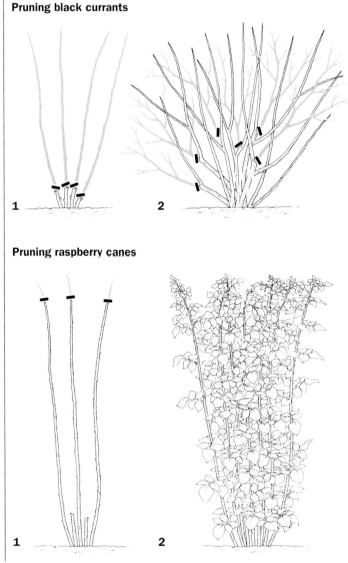

1 2

Pruning raspberry canes

1 2

Greenhouse and windowsill

Watering and ventilation need care now that temperatures are falling. Grey mould or *Botrytis* can be a menace in winter, particularly where there's a combination of a damp, humid atmosphere and low temperatures. Good greenhouse hygiene and ventilation can prevent it becoming a severe problem.

Pick off dead or faded leaves, and space plants out to allow good air movement around the foliage. If any signs of grey mould do appear, remove all the affected parts of the plant and put them in the dustbin – not on the compost heap or you'll be spreading the spores. Spray remaining plants with copper fungicide, which will help prevent the spread of disease.

Before watering, stand the full watering can in the greenhouse for a few hours so the water can warm up. Do the same with compost before sowing seeds or potting up young plants. Plant growth will slow down a lot, so take care to water sparingly. Remove, dry and store capillary matting if you didn't do it last month, as it holds lots of moisture and will make the atmosphere too humid.

Ventilate the greenhouse as much as you can during the day while still maintaining temperatures, and close up at night. If you're heating with paraffin or gas, there needs to be a tiny bit of ventilation at all times. Clean out the greenhouse and insulate ready for winter if you didn't do it last month (see page 153). Check that all the glass is secure and replace any cracked or damaged panes. Give wooden framed structures a coat of preservative if necessary.

CHECKLIST

- Harvest apples and pears; store undamaged fruits.
- Plant spring bulbs. Tulips can now be planted.
- Fix grease bands to apple trees if you have not already done so.
- Lift, divide and replant old clumps of rhubarb.
- Propagate fruit bushes like black currants by hardwood cuttings.
- Prepare a site for asparagus to be planted next spring by digging in plenty of manure.
- Sow broad beans outdoors in mild areas or on light soils.
- Bend cauliflower leaves over the curds to protect them from frost.
- Sow winter lettuce under cloches, in coldframe or greenhouse.
- Sow hardy annuals for spring pot plants.
- Plant lily bulbs in pots in the cold greenhouse.
- Buy material like bubble polythene to have ready for protecting shrubs and containers from severe frosts.
- Finish planting evergreens by the end of the month.
- Move frost-tender shrubs in containers into the greenhouse.

*Dead leaves are a prime target for grey mould (*Botrytis*), so remove them as soon as possible.*

NOVEMBER

SOME GARDENERS say that this is the end of the season, but really it should be looked upon as the beginning. There's no doubt that work done now will lay the foundations for a great garden next season.

Get the digging done, have a really good clean-up, order your seeds, finish new plantings where you can and, above all, go round the borders and correct your mistakes. We all make them and now's the time to put them right.

There's still all the summer's warmth in the soil, so plants that you move will get away quickly. So start with the big plants and take as much soil with them as you can. When they're replanted, pay special attention to the staking. Then mulch round the plant and water well – and that means for the whole of next season too.

◀ *Trees and shrubs with richly-coloured autumn foliage make a wonderful display to bring the season to a close.*

GARDENS TO VISIT

- **Capel Manor Horticultural Centre**, Hertfordshire. Large collection of display gardens with different designs and materials. Large walled garden. Mature shrub borders, woodland areas and water features. Trial grounds of *Gardening Which*.
- **Dundee University Botanic Garden**. Relatively young botanic garden with good collections of trees and shrubs. Tropical and temperate plant houses. Good visitor centre.
- **Hillier Arboreteum**, Hampshire. One of the finest collections of trees and shrubs in Britain. Over 40,000 plants in 11,000 different varieties. Spectacular autumn leaves and berries. Many interesting plants all year.
- **Stourhead**, Wiltshire. One of the greatest landscaped gardens in the country, created 1740–80. Beautiful lakes, many grand architectural features such as temples. Excellent autumn colour from many rare and mature trees.

Looking good

Berries and fruits provide cheerful splashes of colour in the garden once the leaves begin to fall. Some of the shrub roses are terrific, laden with large red or orange hips, like 'Fru Dagmar Hastrup', 'Scabrosa' and 'Scarlet Fire'. Some of the rose species like *Rosa rugosa*, dog rose (*R. canina*), sweet briar (*R. eglanteria*) and *R. moyesii* also bear many hips, though they do form big vigorous bushes which are best sited in a large border or a semi-wild garden. They can also be planted as an informal hedge.

Several small berry-bearing shrubs require a male and female plant to produce berries. *Skimmias* form rounded domes of glossy evergreen foliage and they bear bright red, long-lasting berries. *S. japonica reevesiana* is particularly useful because it produces male and female flowers on the same plant, so one plant will do. It holds its deep sealing-wax-red berries right through winter. Skimmias need a neutral or acid soil, as do *Pernettya mucronata* varieties which have white, ruby-red, pale or dark pink berries. *Viburnum davidii* has striking, bright turquoise-blue, egg-shaped berries, but you'd need several bushes to get adequate pollination.

The gladwyn iris (*I. foetidissima*) is a gem of a plant to cheer up a shady corner. It forms a neat clump of spiky evergreen leaves, and in autumn the swollen seed heads burst open to reveal masses of bright orange berries. Don't be put off by its other common name of 'stinking iris'. When the leaves are crushed, they have a pleasant smell of roast beef!

Shrubs with unusual berries include *Callicarpa bodinieri* 'Profusion' with masses of small, deep lilac-pink berries. *Clerodendrum trichotomum* has bright blue ones which are maroon at the base. Flowering nutmeg (*Leycesteria formosa*) bears dangling clusters of claret-red berries. They're popular with pheasants, hence its other name of pheasant berry.

Coloured or patterned stems are revealed in their full glory as the leaves fall. Attractive bark is often overlooked, but it stands out marvellously in the comparative bareness of a winter garden. Good willows (*Salix*) include scarlet willow (*S. alba* 'Britzensis') with glowing orange-red stems and golden willow (*S.a. vitellina*) that has bright yellow ones. They need hard pruning in spring to keep them as bushes and encourage lots of new colourful stems. The same applies to dogwoods (*Cornus alba* varieties) like 'Sibirica' (dark red) and 'Kesselringii' (dark purple). For a large informal border, ornamental brambles (*Rubus*) like *R. cockburnianus* and *R. thibetanus* have striking white stems. Plant them in front of a hedge or fence for the best effect.

CREATE A KNOT GARDEN

Designs for long thin gardens are easy to find. But for some reason the thousands of new gardeners with a short wide plot are left in the dark. It's a familiar anguished cry that lands in my postbag more often than I would like.

Well, one thing you can do is to make two gardens out of one. In other words, square off the plot to leave one side cut off by perhaps a low hedge or, say, a wattle fence or a length of climber-covered trellis. Then use the cut-off bit to build a formal knot garden. In fact, this traditional type of design is ideal for most small gardens, whatever their shape, as it can be fitted into a very small space.

Mark out a series of squares, diamonds, curved beds or a mixture of shapes, with paths between. The only rule is that they should be strictly geometric. Then edge the beds with a low-growing hedge. The most popular is dwarf box, but you could use lavender, rosemary, santolina or dwarf berberis. Really, anything low-growing that will clip into a formal hedge will do. Inside the box, plant with herbs or low-growing cottage-garden flowers. It's an expensive job, I'm afraid, because the hedging is not cheap, but if you have patience, you could grow your own from half-ripe cuttings (see page 120). It takes time, of course, but you get a lovely warm glow of satisfaction at the end.

General tasks

Bird boxes should be cleaned of old nesting material which can harbour parasites. Wash them out with boiling water and repair them if necessary. Do this job well before late winter, when some birds will already be prospecting for nest sites.

Borders can be weeded and tidied at any time through the winter, so long as the soil is dry enough not to stick to your boots. Cut back the dead stems of perennials, chop them up and add them to the compost heap. Rake fallen leaves off plants, and either collect them to make leafmould or leave them on bare ground to rot down. Dig up and compost annual weeds, but burn or throw away the roots of perennial ones.

Protect delicate plants that can suffer in frosty weather, like cistus, fuchsias and penstemons, by tucking bracken or straw around their bases. Don't use peat or compost as these materials hold water and rot the plant.

Hedgehogs and toads often crawl into heaps of garden rubbish, particularly leaves, to hibernate for the winter, so check bonfires before setting fire to them. Hedgehogs tend to hibernate in compost heaps, so take a little care as you fork out the compost or turn it. When you're building a new heap, make a deluxe hedgehog home at the bottom: use an old washing-up bowl turned upside-down with a hole cut in the side and, leading from this, a piece of old drainpipe as an entrance tunnel.

Plant both container-grown and bare-rooted plants as described on page 144 so long as the ground isn't soaking wet or frozen. Plant winter-flowering heathers now for a good display of flowers from December to March.

Snow in large amounts can damage garden plants and structures. Conifers that have a narrow fastigiate habit, like *Juniperus* 'Skyrocket', can be loosely wrapped with wire or netting so that their branches aren't forced out of shape. Make sure that the roofs of garden buildings are sound. Take the netting roof off the fruit cage, but replace it with large-mesh netting if bullfinches are likely to be a problem.

PLANTING TULIPS

Unlike most spring bulbs, tulips are best planted in late autumn, because they can be susceptible to disease if they're planted earlier.

On heavy, poorly drained soils, give bulbs extra protection against rotting, by planting them on a layer of coarse grit. This ensures the vulnerable base plant will stay dry.

1 *Dig out the planting hole to around 15 cm (6 in) deep, and put in a layer of coarse grit approximately 5 cm (2 in) deep.*

2 *Set the bulbs out in a natural-looking group, allowing about 7.5 cm (3 in) between each one, then backfill the hole with soil and firm it gently.*

Ornamental garden

BULBS

Nerines and other slightly tender, bulbous plants like *Agapanthus* that remain in the ground all winter benefit from a thick mulch of straw or bark in colder areas.

Most spring-flowering bulbs should have been planted by now, though tulips can go in up to the end of the month. Late planting also has the advantage of generally avoiding the disease tulip fire.

HERBACEOUS PERENNIALS AND ALPINES

Alpines with woolly or fleshy leaves dislike winter wet. Cover them with a small cloche or a pane of glass to keep off the worst of the rain. *Lewisias* really benefit from protection as they detest water lying in their rosettes of leaves – planting them at an angle also helps to prevent waterlogging. Christmas rose (*Helleborus niger*) also benefits from protection.

*Many shrub roses produce glowing red hips in autumn. These look lovely against a silver-leaved cotton lavender (*Santolina*).*

SHRUBS

Hardwood cuttings taken last year should be carefully lifted and moved to a nursery bed or potted up. Grow them on for a further year before planting them out into well-prepared soil.

Protect shrubs from winter damage. Stake or tie in evergreen shrubs if necessary to prevent them from wind-rocking. Check the ties on all plants are secure and in no danger of rubbing. Mulch rhododendrons with chipped bark or compost to protect their shallow roots from frost damage.

PLANT OF THE MONTH

Crab apple (*Malus* 'Evereste')
HEIGHT: 4 m (13 ft)
SPREAD: 3 m (10 ft)
FLOWERING TIME: April–May
POSITION: Any
SOIL: Any **HARDY?**: Yes

All crab apples are excellent small garden trees, but 'Evereste' is particularly outstanding. Its habit is neat and rounded, and in spring it's covered in large blossoms, red in bud opening to white tinged with pink. In autumn masses of bright orange-yellow fruit are produced, and they stay on the tree to provide colour for months, often into the new year. Even when they drop, they serve to feed wild birds.

Kitchen garden

FRUIT

New fruit trees and bushes are best planted this month, as soon as the new season's crop is available.

Varieties of soft fruit with some disease resistance are by far the best, as you don't need to spray these with fungicides. Gooseberry 'Invicta' and 'Jubilee', and black currant 'Ben More' and 'Ben Lomond' have good resistance to mildew.

Soft fruit is losing ground in many gardens through lack of space, though there are lots of ways to get a quart out of a pint pot. Choose compact heavy-cropping bushes like black currants 'Ben Sarek' which can be planted only 1 m (3 ft) apart. Gooseberries can be grown as cordons – single shoots trained upwards on horizontal wires spaced 30 cm (1 ft) apart with 30 cm (1 ft) between each plant. The side shoots are pruned in summer to create short fruiting spurs (see page 137). They're also available as standards, like a bush on a 1.2-m (4-ft) stem, so you can grow them in the flower borders and strawberries can be grown underneath.

Briar fruits can be grown on post-and-wire supports, either within the garden or as an unusual boundary. Use 1.8-m (6-ft) posts with strong galvanized wires strung horizontally at 30-cm (1-ft) intervals. Thornless varieties may be best where space is limited, like loganberry 'LY 654' and blackberry 'Merton Thornless'. Summer-fruiting raspberries are also grown on similar supports but with wires 45 cm (1½ ft) apart. Plant the canes 45 cm (1½ ft) apart. Immediately after planting, prune raspberries back to 30 cm (1 ft) from the ground, and prune all black currants shoots back to ground level. This will encourage lots of new vigorous shoots next spring.

See page 104 for details of growing fruit trees in a small space.

VEGETABLES

Broad beans and peas can be sown outside or under cloches. Choose early varieties such as broad bean 'Aquadulce Claudia' or 'Aquadulce Loreta', and pea 'Daybreak', 'Douce Provence' or 'Feltham First'. However, there's little advantage over spring-sown crops. See page 16 for spacings.

Outdoor crops can be covered with cloches, either temporarily to protect them during periods of severe frost, or permanently to encourage an earlier crop. There are many different ready-made cloches on sale made from glass, rigid plastic and polythene, though a cheap and cheerful alternative is to make your own tunnel cloche with a long piece of clear polythene. Stretch it over wire loops made from coathangers, and secure the polythene by burying it in the soil at each end. Cloches are also very useful in spring to bring on crops early.

THE GARDEN INDOORS

PERENNIALS FOR INDOOR COLOUR

One of the beauties of perennials is that, unlike most plants, they positively enjoy being dug up and replanted every few years. Many early-flowering varieties can make wonderful pot plants if they're lifted and potted now, and brought under cover where they'll flower through the winter.

Earliest to flower is the Christmas rose (*Helleborus niger*) with its beautiful pure white flowers. Double-flowered primroses often flower in winter and their intricate blooms, that look almost like porcelain, can be fully appreciated at close quarters. Many spring-flowering perennials can be lifted and brought into flower early, like drumstick primulas (*Primula denticulata*), *P. rosea* 'Grandiflora', polyanthus, lily-of-the-valley (*Convallaria*), elephant's ears (*Bergenia*) and kingcup (*Caltha palustris*).

Dig up the plants carefully and pot them into 10–18-cm (4–7-in) containers, depending on their size. Bring them under cover, either into a greenhouse, porch, conservatory or windowsill, in gentle heat. Keep the soil moist and feed weekly during flowering.

Greenhouse and windowsill

Heating is now usually essential if you want to keep the greenhouse frost-free. A thermostatically-controlled electric heater is the most convenient to use, though there are also paraffin and propane gas heaters if you don't have an electricity supply. There should be a small but constant amount of ventilation if you're using gas or paraffin. It's definitely worth installing bubble polythene insulation to save both fuel and money.

A large greenhouse is obviously costly to heat. Save on fuel by sorting out those plants that need most warmth and put them to one end of the greenhouse. Separate them off with a curtain of bubble polythene and insulate this section well, so that only this area is heated to the necessary higher temperature.

Coldframes can also be insulated with bubble polythene and even kept frost-free with a small heater or a soil-warming cable. During really cold weather, protect plants even further by covering the whole frame with a piece of old carpet.

Bubble polythene can easily be fixed to the inside of the greenhouse with plastic clips. It'll give your plants extra protection and save a lot of money on your heating bills.

CHECKLIST

- Continue taking hardwood cuttings of shrubs and fruit bushes.
- Inspect potted bulbs regularly and water sparingly if necessary.
- Feed flowering pot plants weekly with a liquid fertilizer.
- Plant spring bedding and winter pansies by the end of the month.
- Lift and store dahlia tubers as soon as possible.
- Twist off dead indoor cyclamen leaves and flowers where they join the corm: remaining pieces of stem can cause it to rot.
- Pinch out the tips of autumn-sown sweet peas when they're about 10 cm (4 in) high.
- Check that tree ties are securely fitted and in no danger of rubbing.
- Put guards round young trees if there's any danger of rabbit or deer damage.
- Give wild-flower meadows a final cut so that the spring flowers can be seen at their best.
- Drain hosepipes, roll them up and store under cover.
- Lag outdoor pipes and taps to prevent them freezing, drain them if possible.
- Order seed catalogues.
- Clean pots and seedtrays with hot water and disinfectant, ready for next spring.
- Plant garlic by the end of the month.
- Force seakale either indoors or outdoors.
- Lift and force witloof chicory (see page 89).
- Check stored fruit and vegetables; throw out any showing signs of rot.
- Net Brussels and cabbage to protect them from birds.
- Prune bush apple and pear trees, and black currants (see pages 164 and 180).
- Stop feeding fish as they'll live off their reserves for the winter months.

DECEMBER

I N MY EXPERIENCE December is a marvellous month in the garden. The weather's often not at all bad, so work can continue, but with time to plan, and to dream just a little too. It's a month for new ideas and for change. So if something simply isn't going to work, admit it, look at it afresh and come up with a solution.

If, for example, there's a bit of grass that's too shaded to grow anything but moss, dig it up and plant shade-loving plants. If there's a tree or a shrub in the wrong place, move it or pull it out: but plant another one (or two) somewhere else, though always check with the local council before cutting down an older tree in case there's a preservation order on it.

◄ *It's worth not cutting back the dead stems of herbaceous perennials so they can be transformed with a silvering of frost.*

GARDENS TO VISIT

- **Bicton College of Agriculture**, Devon. Magnificent tender perennials for summer colour. Glasshouses with tender plants. Arboretum looks especially good in spring and autumn, plus beautiful trees in parkland setting. Plant centre.
- **Edinburgh Botanic Garden**. Ten landscaped glasshouses with a huge range of exotic plants. World-famous rock garden is particularly good in spring/early summer. Woodland garden and arboretum. Shop, café, plants for sale.
- **Harlow Carr Botanical Gardens**, Yorkshire. Gardens of the Northern Horticultural Society. Landscaped with many attractive features and themed areas including alpines, heathers, roses, fruit and vegetable plots. Study centre, museum, restaurant, shop and plant centre.
- **Wisley Gardens**, Surrey. Headquarters of the Royal Horticultural Society. Formal water garden, glasshouses, huge rock garden, herbaceous borders, alpine houses, rose gardens, demonstration gardens, woodland and wild areas. Extensive plant centre, shop, café and restaurant.

Looking good

Evergreens are star performers in the winter garden. During the summer they fade, acting as a foil for the many different flowering plants, but once deciduous shrubs have shed their leaves and perennials have died back, their foliage really does come into its own.

Golden-variegated leaves make a real splash of sunshine on gloomy days. Aucubas like *A. japonica* 'Crotonifolia' and 'Picturata' look terrific in the back of the border, while hollies (*Ilex*) like 'Golden King' and 'Golden Queen' slowly form large shrubs which can be clipped to shape if desired. *Escallonia* 'Gold Brian' is a showy shrub with incredibly bright leaves, though it needs a sheltered site. Easiest to grow of all, and often unfairly despised because of its green-leaved rampant cousin, is golden privet (*Ligustrum ovalifolium*

'Aureum'), which can be left to form a tall shrub, clipped to shape or even trained as a standard.

Plants with white-and-green variegated leaves are more muted but just as cheering in winter as gold. The ultra-prickly silver hedgehog holly (*Ilex aquifolium* 'Ferox Argentea') and *I.a.* 'Argentea Marginata' are two excellent variegated hollies. Some shrubs have holly-like foliage, such as *Osmanthus* 'Goshiki' with dark green leaves splashed with white. Others have tiny leaves, like *Lonicera nitida* 'Silver Beauty' which could be grown as a low hedge. *Viburnum tinus* 'Variegatum' has creamy-yellow and green leaves, which look good with its winter clusters of pink-tinged flowers, though it needs a sheltered site in colder areas.

Ivies (*Hedera*) are anything but dull. Cover a wall with the cream-and-green large-leaved variety *Hedera colchica* 'Dentata Variegata', or with 'Sulphur Heart' which has greenish-yellow and dark green foliage, and you'll brighten up the whole garden. They look superb all year and they also tolerate poor soil and total shade. What more can you ask?

Conifers add winter colour and structure to a mixed border with shrubs, perennials and other plants. There are greens, blues and golds, and there's an enormous range of shapes and sizes from tiny dwarfs to 10-m (30-ft) specimens. They all look pretty innocuous when they're young, so do remember to check their eventual height before buying!

Winter flowers look almost too fragile to withstand the harsh weather, but most shrubs are surprisingly tough. A few winter blossoms from plants like *Viburnum bodnantense*, winter jasmine, wintersweet and Christmas box will give your spirits a much-needed boost when the weather's cold and dreary. See page 12 and 20 for more details.

MAKING A PLANT-FILLED PATH

Paths are necessary in the garden but take up an unacceptable amount of space in a small plot. The solution is to use the path itself to grow plants.

Start by installing wooden edging. Use 75 x 25-mm (3 x 1-in) timber that has been pressure treated with preservative and fix it to pegs made of the same material. A good width for a small garden is 60 cm (2 ft) to take 45-cm- (1½-ft)-square slabs. Dig out between the edgings to 10 cm (4 in) deep, retaining the best of the topsoil. Mix this with equal parts of coarse grit or pea-shingle and coir compost and replace it. Rake it out level and tread it down firmly. Then rake it again and lay the paving slabs on top so that they're equidistant from either side, with the same distance between the slabs. With a 60-cm- (2-ft)-wide path, that'll leave 7.5 cm (3 in) either side. Tap them down as firmly as you can with the handle of a 3-lb hammer so that they finish level with the top of the wooden edging. When all the slabs are laid, plant up with spreading alpine plants like thymes, aubrieta, alyssum and so on, then mulch around them with more of the coarse grit. Gradually the plants will spread to make a very attractive path – though you'll have to take care walking down it!

General tasks

Deciduous hedges that are overgrown can be pruned any time during winter. Cut the hedge 30–60 cm (1–2 ft) lower than the height you actually want, to allow space for the new growth. Shape the hedge for stability: narrower at the top and wider at the base. New deciduous hedges are best planted during late autumn/early winter when bare-rooted plants are available, as container-grown ones are much more expensive. Look out for cell-grown plants which already have a good fibrous root system – they're sold in packs of five or ten.

Immediately after planting cut back the plants to 10 cm (6 in) from the ground to encourage lots of strong bushy growth next year.

Feeding birds has benefits both ways. It can mean the difference between life and death in cold weather, and in return they'll eat many garden pests. They're also fascinating to watch and their daily antics will soon have you hooked. Do remember that they'll come to depend on the food you put out and could starve to death without it, so you must continue to feed them daily until spring. Peanuts are a sure-fire favourite, but don't buy damp or mouldy ones as they could contain a poisonous fungus called aflatoxin. Fruit, seeds and meat scraps are all welcome. Make kitchen scraps into bird cake by mixing them with melted lard. Harmful foods to avoid at all costs are salty or spicy foods, and desiccated coconut which swells up in the birds' stomachs. Too much dry bread has the same effect, so soak it in water first. A regular supply of water is also vital during freezing weather for drinking and bathing. A shallow dish or even an upturned dustbin lid is ideal.

Frost and wind can lift and loosen new plants which allows ice to form around the stem. Check them every couple of weeks and refirm them if necessary.

Ensure that tree ties are secure and that they're not rubbing the trunk. If you need emergency ties, old nylon tights are an excellent temporary measure as they're strong, flexible and won't rub the bark.

Stored bulbs, fruit, vegetables and tubers should all be checked every few weeks. Throw out any showing signs of rot, which can quickly spread. Make sure that the compost around dahlias and other tubers isn't allowed to dry out completely.

Winter is a good time to plan what to grow next year. It's a great idea to keep a garden diary, then you can look back on your successes as well as your mistakes. It will also be a very useful memory-jogger for garden jobs in future years.

Provided there's no frost in the ground, shrubs can still be planted. But, if the soil's wet, be careful not to overfirm or it'd be like setting the roots in concrete.

Ornamental garden

HERBACEOUS PERENNIALS AND ALPINES

Alpines and other seeds that need a cold period in order to germinate should be sown now. Sow the seeds thinly in small pots or trays of compost made up of equal parts of soil, coarse grit and coir compost. Large seeds can be 'chipped' with a sharp knife so water can break through the hard seed coat. Cover the seed with a 1-cm-(½-in)-thick layer of coarse grit, which will protect the seeds from too

▶ *There are still plenty of plants to brighten the winter garden. The bare, red stems of dogwoods (*Cornus alba *'Sibirica') and the golden conifer foliage, glow with colour when they're touched by the winter sunlight.*

much rain and prevent the growth of moss and weeds. Stand the pots in a coldframe or a sheltered spot outside.

The seeds may take months or, in some cases, more than a year to germinate, so do be patient and don't throw the contents of the pots away too quickly. Remember to label each pot with a long-lasting tag, marked with the plant name and the date of sowing.

PLANT OF THE MONTH

***Elaeagnus x ebbingei* 'Gilt Edge'**
HEIGHT: 1.8-2.4 m (6-8 ft)
SPREAD: 1.2-1.8 m (4-6 ft)
POSITION: Sun/part shade.
SOIL: Any **HARDY?**: Yes

Evergreens like elaeagnus are part of the essential 'skeleton' of the winter garden, and at other times of the year they make an excellent backdrop for flowering plants. Brightest of all is 'Gilt Edge' with its green and gold leaves. Other good varieties include E. 'Coastal Gold and *E. pungens* 'Maculata'. For extra summer colour, try growing a blue-flowering clematis like C. x *durandii* through an elaeagnus—its gold foliage makes a wonderful backcloth for the deep blue flowers.

Kitchen garden

FRUIT

Bush apple and pear trees can be pruned through winter while they're dormant, though it's best to complete pruning by the end of the year if possible.

Older ones that have formed dense heads of branches need to be thinned to let light and air through the tree. First take out any damaged or crossing branches, and remove any wood that is diseased. Take off the the tips of shoots that have been shrivelled by mildew – make sure you burn them or throw them out so the disease spores don't spread. Then thin out the remaining ones if necessary. When cutting large branches, make a small cut with the saw through the underside, so that it doesn't fall and tear a long strip of bark off the trunk.

Always use a sharp pruning saw, and remove complete branches or cut back to a strong joint. Take care not to leave a long stump of wood which will eventually die back and become diseased. Any pruning cuts larger than 5 cm (2 in) across should be painted with a special pruning paint which helps prevent disease entering through the fresh cuts. However, it's best not to paint over the very centre of the stump.

VEGETABLES

Witloof chicory can be forced from December to April to produce fresh crisp 'chicons' (tight buds of young leaves). Dig up the roots from the garden and cut off the tops to leave about 2.5 cm (1 in) of stem. It's best to lift all the roots at once and store them in damp sand or soil until required, as they can be attacked by pests if they're left in the ground.

Select a few roots and trim the thin end if they're over-long. Put the roots upright in a deep box of moist soil, garden compost or bark, so that the tops are about 23 cm (9 in) below the surface. Keep the box in a warm place and check it regularly to make sure the soil hasn't dried out. In about five to six weeks' time, dig down gently: you should find that each root has formed a good 'chicon' on top.

Alternatively treat the roots as for seakale (see page 164) and put them in a deep pot with an inverted pot or bucket on top to keep out the light. Remember to block the drainage holes with a little clay or putty so every bit of light is excluded.

THE GARDEN INDOORS

MAKING A CHRISTMAS WREATH

Christmas can be an expensive time, but you can save money and have an original decoration into the bargain by using material from your garden to make a handsome wreath for your front door.

YOU'LL NEED:
A frame of strong wire to make a circle 30–38 cm (12–15 in) across. Special frames can be bought from florists, or make your own with galvanized wire or even a coathanger. Moss to clothe the frame. Green garden twine. Thin garden wire or florist's wire. The plant material can be varied according to what's available. Use evergreen foliage like Leyland cypress, holly (both green and variegated), bunches of berries or hips for colour, and fir cones or beech mast for decoration.

First make the wire into a hoop. Tie the end of the twine on to the wire and cover the frame with damp moss, securing it by wrapping the string round and round the moss. Cut a piece of thin wire, tie a few sprigs of green foliage together with it and secure them to the frame by threading the wire through the moss. Continue to tie on bunches of foliage until the whole frame is covered.

Then add the decorative material like bunches of berries, variegated foliage and fir cones, securing them in the same way. The fruit or berries could come from crab apples, cotoneasters, shrub roses or gladwyn iris. Spray the clusters of fruits with hair lacquer or clear varnish so that they'll be less likely to drop. A wide bow of red ribbon can be added to the bottom of the wreath as a final decorative and seasonal touch.

Greenhouse and windowsill

Bulbs that are stored in the dark for forcing should be inspected regularly. Check that the compost has not dried out and water it sparingly if necessary. Take care not to over-water or the bulbs could rot.

When the tips of the leaves are 2.5–5 cm (1–2 in) above the compost, move the bulbs out of the dark to a greenhouse or a cool windowsill at a temperature of around 10°C (50°F). Once the leaves are around 10 cm (4 in) high, move the pots to a warmer room or raise the temperature to around 18°C (64°F).

Grape vines in the greenhouse can be pruned once the leaves have fallen. Cut back the side shoots to leave one good bud and take a third of this year's growth off the main stem.

Houseplants are favourite Christmas presents, but sadly some of them don't even make it beyond Twelfth Night. The most popular ones – cyclamen, poinsettias and azaleas – all have differing requirements. Cyclamen need good light and cool conditions. When watering, avoid splashing water on the corm. It's best to stand the plant in a saucer of water for an hour. Poinsettias like a warm room and they need to be kept moist, but they dislike being waterlogged. It's difficult to keep poinsettias for more than one season because they need a carefully managed day-length regime to flower next year. Azaleas detest a hot dry atmosphere and especially central heating. They should never be allowed to dry out, and they prefer a cool position on a windowsill or in a porch or conservatory.

Regularly go through the greenhouse every week or so and have a quick tidy-up. Remove and dispose of dead leaves and flowers, and water plants sparingly – do so in the mornings so that the moisture dries off the foliage quickly. This all helps keep disease at bay. Remember that over-wintering plants, such as tender

SOWING GERANIUMS

1 *Sow the seed thinly onto a pot of moist coir compost. It helps to sow the seeds from a fold of paper, which can be tapped gently to disperse the seeds equally.*

2 *Cover the seeds with a little fine compost, putting it through a sieve first.*

3 *Cover the pot with a sheet of glass to keep the compost moist. Water by standing in a saucer rather than watering from the top, to avoid washing the fine seed deep into the compost. Keep at 18°C (64°F).*

perennials, need to be kept on the dry side. They tolerate the cold far better if they've got dry feet. Keep an eye out for pests like vine weevil (see page 73). Wash the greenhouse glass if it's covered with green algae to make the most of every bit of scarce winter light.

▼ *When watering cyclamen, take care not to splash water onto the corm, as this could cause it to rot. Remember that cyclamen need regular watering and feeding, especially after the flowers have finished.*

▲ *Make the most of the meagre winter light by washing the greenhouse glass. You'll be surprised how much grime there can be on apparently clean glass.*

▶ *Protected under a blanket of snow, the garden lies dormant through the depths of winter.*

CHECKLIST

- Pick flower buds of *Iris unguicularis* for a vase.
- Prune roses by half to prevent wind-rocking if you did not do so earlier.
- Heel in mail-order plants if they can't be planted within a few days.
- Cover Christmas rose (*Helleborus niger*) with cloches to protect the opening flower buds.
- Take hardwood cuttings of shrubs and fruit bushes.
- Clean moss from paths and patios or they can become dangerously slippery.
- Barrow manure on to the vegetable plot when the ground is frozen – put planks on the lawn so that it doesn't get damaged.
- Put netting over winter greens and fruit bushes to protect them from birds.
- Repair fences and other structures while climbing plants are dormant.
- Feed flowering houseplants weekly with a liquid feed.
- Clean pots and seedtrays, service tools and tidy the garden shed.
- Hoe off weeds during mild dry weather.
- Dig heavy ground during dry weather and leave it rough for frost to break down. It'll also expose pests for birds to eat.
- Plant new trees and shrubs if the weather and ground are favourable.
- Sow broad beans and peas outside or under cloches.

INDEX

Page numbers in *italic* refer to the illustrations

C

G

Gardens of the Rose 95
garlic 124, 152
Gazania 128
Geranium 98
geraniums 28, 48, 101, 132, 181
gladioli 60, *60*, 161
Glasgow Botanic Gardens 11
globe artichokes 49, 89,124
globe flowers 80
gloxinias 21, 47
golden rain tree *74–5*, 76
golden rod *150*, *158–9*
gooseberries 67, 107, 172
grafted trees 57
grape vines 181
grasses, ornamental 58, 140
grease bands 151, *151*
Great Dixter 111
green manure 35, 144
greenfly 104, 121
greenhouses: bulbs in 153
  cleaning 153, *182*
  heating 137, 173
  hygiene 165, 181
  insulating 173, *173*
  in January 17
  pests and diseases 47, 93
  shading 72
  vegetables 48–9, 125
  ventilation 17, 29, 49,125, 165
  watering 165
grey mould 107, 124, 165, *165*
growing bags 153
guelder rose 157
Gunnera manicata 80

H

Halesia carolina 76
hanging baskets 71, 92,101, *102*, 132
hardening off 72
hardwood cuttings 162–3, 171
Harlow Carr Botanical Gardens 175
hazels 34
heathers 42, 56, 64, 169
Hedera 176
hedgehogs 169
hedges: conifer 116
  cutting *85*
  evergreens 62, 85, 116
  pruning *22*, 177
hellebores 20, 104, 170,172
herbs 44, 68, 88, 107, 136, 163
Heuchera 98
Hibiscus syriacus 140
Hillier Arboretum 167
Hippeastrum 47, *47*, 71
Hippophae rhamnoides 157
hoeing 89, 100, *100*
Holcus mollis 'Variegatus' *59*
holidays 116, 127
Holker Hall 127
hollies 176
honeysuckle 97, *103*
houseplants 109, 127, 161, 181
hyacinths 141, *141*
Hydrangea quercifolia 156

IJK

Iberis sempervirens 56
Ilex 176
Impatiens 36, 112–13, 161
Indian bean tree 129
Inverewe 95
Ipomoea 71, 113
irises 20, 33, *78–9*, 98, 103–4, *106*, 113–14, 168
Irishman's cuttings 61
ivies 37, 176

January 11–17
Japanese anemones 157
Jasminum nudiflorum 15, 20, 24
Jasminum officinale 24
Jerusalem artichokes 27
Judas tree 76
July 111–25
June 95–109

Kaffir lilies 158, *158*
kale 70
kingcups *43*, 80
Knightshayes Court 51
Kniphofia 130–1, *142–3*,162
knot gardens 168
kohl rabi 70

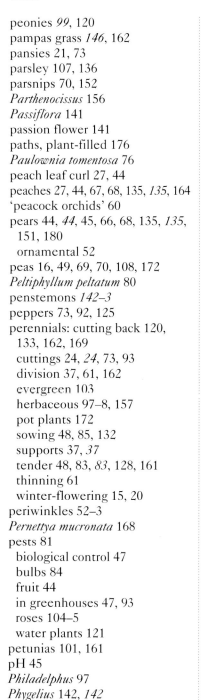

P

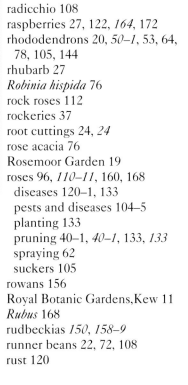

QR

Index